SCALING LEAN

SCALING LEAN

Mastering the Key Metrics for Startup Growth

Ash Maurya

Portfolio / Penguin

PORTFOLIO / PENGUIN
An imprint of Penguin Random House LLC
375 Hudson Street
New York, New York 10014
penguin.com

Library of Congress Cataloging-in-Publication Data

Names: Maurya, Ash, author.
Title: Scaling lean : mastering the key metrics for startup growth / Ash Maurya.
Description: New York : Portfolio/Penguin, [2016]
Identifiers: LCCN 2016017402 | ISBN 9781101980521 (print)
Subjects: LCSH: Business planning. | New business enterprises. | Small business—Growth.
Classification: LCC HD30.28 .M3755 2016 | DDC 658.4/013—dc23 LC record
    available at https://lccn.loc.gov/2016017402

ISBN 9781101980521 (hardcover)
ISBN 9781101980538 (ebook)

Printed in the United States of America
10   9   8   7   6   5   4   3

Set in Kepler Std Light with Geometric
Designed by Daniel Lagin

To Sasha—for constantly helping me see the larger goal.

CONTENTS

PART 2
PRIORITIZING WASTE

PART 3
ACHIEVING BREAKTHROUGH

SCALING LEAN

INTRODUCTION

Another Book About Startup Growth?

ANOTHER BOOK ABOUT STARTUP GROWTH METRICS? WHY ADD TO AN already crowded shelf?

I have had the entrepreneurial bug my whole life. I came to the United States on a student visa which restricted me from starting a company. So I did the next best thing. I joined a telecom startup shortly after graduating from university. After a few false product starts, that startup eventually found product/market fit with a voice-over-IP softswitch product, which led to a successful exit in 2002. That is when I left to launch my first startup, WiredReach. Like the earlier startup, Wired-Reach began with a few false starts until I found product/market fit with a file-sharing product targeted at small businesses. I subsequently sold that business in 2010 to start my latest venture, LeanStack. Our mission is helping entrepreneurs everywhere succeed.

My first book, *Running Lean*, grew out of the first set of challenges I experienced as a startup founder: the need to quickly iterate from an early-stage idea (or plan A) into a plan that works. I had built many products over the years, and while they all started out equally exciting, not all of them stood the test of the market. I realized that I had many more ideas than I had time or resources to test them. More important, I didn't have a repeatable process for doing so.

> Life's too short to build something nobody wants.

This prompted my search for the repeatable metaprocess I describe in *Running Lean*. It was derived from rigorous testing and firsthand experiential learning by building many of my own products and by working alongside hundreds of other entrepreneurs spread across the globe in domains ranging from software to hardware and high-tech to no-tech businesses.

The big epiphany for me while writing and researching *Running Lean* was that the true product of a successful entrepreneur is not just a great solution or an innovative piece of technology, but a repeatable process that connects your solution with paying customers—in other words, finding a working business model.

But it turns out that's not enough. *Running Lean*, though it delivered on its promise, described only the first step in a two-step process on the path to building a successful startup. Over time I found that when the time came to scale up my products and teams, my most rigorously tested business models faced a whole new set of challenges. I learned firsthand that seemingly watertight business models can disintegrate under the pressures of expanding into new markets and managing stakeholder expectations.

I went searching for a solution.

Scale Starts with Metrics

Building a scalable and successful business starts with knowing what to measure and how.

The first and most important stakeholder in the business is you, and your scarcest resource is time. Every minute spent on a business that is doomed to fail is a waste, and so it's critical for you to be able to identify—quickly, early, and accurately— whether a business idea is worth pursuing.

What's more, you're going to be called on to demonstrate progress to external shareholders. From the earliest days of a startup's life, you as a founder have to justify your new venture's "potential for progress" to a VC, CFO, spouse, or even yourself as a prerequisite to securing runway.

Early-stage startups typically rely on two measures of progress: how much stuff they are building and how much money they are making. Yet unfortunately, both of these metrics are unreliable proxies of progress that can lead you down the wrong path—building something nobody wants.

Traditional accounting metrics, like revenue, profit, and return on investment (ROI), aren't helpful at the early stages because they all track numbers that are negative or near zero. Even at later stages, relying solely on aggregate revenue can prevent you from uncovering the right growth strategies.

When my businesses were at this stage, I found myself wanting to collect and analyze as much data as possible. But in a world where we can measure almost anything, it's easy to drown in a sea of nonactionable data. I learned how to keep from drowning—and how to navigate the unfamiliar terrain that comes after *Running Lean*.

> You are the first investor in your business idea. You invest with time, which is more valuable than money.

The Wrong Way to Do It

Take a typical startup founder—let's call him Bob. He has a great idea for a business. This is the "honeymoon period" of his venture when anything seems possible. Bob believes it would be more effective to first build out his solution and make it easier for others to see his vision. Halfway through, he realizes that he underestimated the scope of his solution and decides he needs to secure additional resources to continue.

> This book will teach you the metrics that define a working business model. Armed with these metrics, you can justify the investment of your time and communicate progress with your internal and external stakeholders—without drowning in a sea of numbers.

Bob spends the next several weeks writing a sixty-page business plan. He knows that the trick is starting with the right "exit number" and then working backward.

The right exit number represents the return on investment he needs to promise his investors. This number needs to be big enough to whet their appetite, but also within the realm of believability to maximize his odds of getting funded. There is a running joke in business schools that the best spreadsheets get funded. So Bob labors endlessly on his forecasts, often made up of hundreds of numbers. Then he hits the pitching circuit to raise funding for his idea.

After several additional months of pitching and lots of rejection, he manages to raise just enough seed capital to move forward.

Bob hires a team and spends the next several months tracking progress against the execution of his plan. Because revenue is nonexistent during this phase of the venture, Bob settles for measuring progress by ensuring that his team is building their product on schedule and within budget.

Fast-forward a year. Bob's team has been very busy and managed to launch their product to market. But while they have some revenue to show, they have missed their projected targets—by a lot. Under pressure to demonstrate more promising revenue numbers to his stakeholders, Bob resorts to a number of short-term accounting tactics and product strategies, such as taking on custom development projects. These provide a temporary Band-Aid to the revenue problem, distracting him further from building a repeatable and scalable business model.

Because all the money is now spent, Bob goes back to his stakeholders and attempts to pitch a brand-new vision that promises an even bigger exit. All he needs is a larger team and ten times more money.

You know how this story ends, right? Bob is fired.

Starting Right, Still Ending Wrong

Mary too has an idea for a business, but she takes a "lean" approach to starting up. She knows that the top reason products fail is not a failure to build out the product, but rather a failure to build a *repeatable* and *scalable* business model.

She intends to navigate her entrepreneurial journey by following the three-step metaprocess outlined in *Running Lean:*

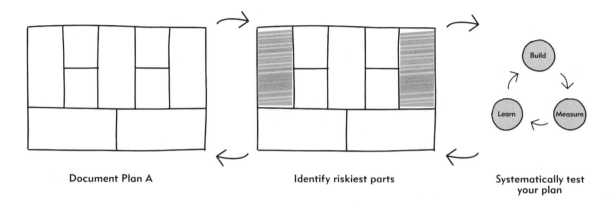

Document Plan A   Identify riskiest parts   Systematically test
your plan

Rather than spending weeks writing a full-fledged business plan or rushing to build out her solution, she quickly sketches her business model using a tool like the one-page Lean Canvas worksheet.* This lets her quickly deconstruct her vision and, better yet, capture her business model on a single page that she can share with other potential team members, advisers, and investors.

She has valuable conversations about her business model, conversations that help her identify the riskiest assumptions in her thinking. She then gets outside the building and begins stress testing her riskiest assumptions through a series of small and fast experiments. Finally, Mary synthesizes everything she learns in order to define the first iteration of her solution, or minimum viable product (MVP).

Compared with Bob, Mary got started much faster. With the backing of early customer validation, she is also on a more solid footing. Her early customer validation paves the way for securing additional resources from her stakeholders to move forward. But that's when her problems begin.

---

* You can download a Lean Canvas worksheet at http://leanstack.com/lean-canvas.

While it was easy for Mary to pinpoint her starting risks, things get a lot murkier after her company launches its MVP. Her company is now signing up dozens of users a day, but conversions to paying customers are well below projected targets. There is no way her team can talk to every user as Mary had done during the early days of the company. Her team decides to invest in metrics to understand what's going wrong.

Drowning in Numbers

Mary's team starts off with a few simple off-the-shelf tools and supplements them with their own homegrown dashboards. Pretty soon they are tracking thousands of different data points. Then they get that drowning feeling.

"In God we trust. All others bring data."

—W. EDWARDS DEMING

The problem with metrics is that while they can tell you what's going wrong, they can't tell you why.

You don't need lots of numbers, but a few key actionable metrics.

Suboptimal Experiments

Mary's team is simultaneously running all kinds of experiments. But despite using a lot of jargon in their team meetings, like "hypotheses," "learning," and "pivots," her team is unable to change the fact that their sales numbers plot into a discouraging line.

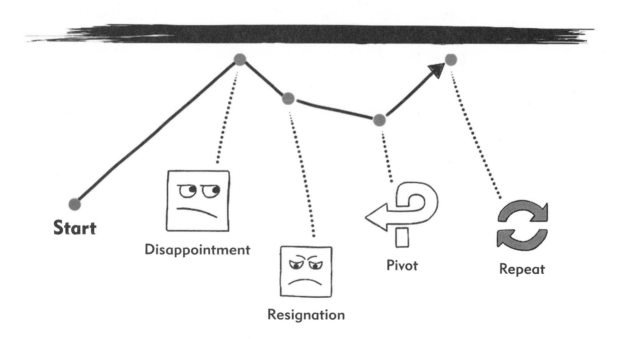

Start

Disappointment

Resignation

Pivot

Repeat

The Curse of Specialization

While running experiments is a key activity in the Lean Canvas business model, you have to know how to design them for breakthrough learning.

Mary intuits that she needs to slow down and refocus. She reorganizes her team into departments and assigns each one a set of core metrics tied to their performance and compensation structure. Her sales team is tracked on accounts closed, her marketing team on leads generated, and her development team on product quality metrics.

This has an unintended effect. While these department-level key performance indicators (KPIs) were designed to drive focus and optimize for overall organizational throughput, they started having the opposite effect. For instance, sales quotas were typically met in the last week of the month. But while more deals were being closed, customer cancellations (or churn) started going up. The marketing team generated hundreds of additional leads by spending their entire budget, but the overall conversion to paying customers wasn't going up. And developers were busier than ever building more features at an incredible pace. But customer retention and satisfaction were actually going down, not up. What was going on?

Money Talks

When all else fails, one can always fall back on revenue as a measure of progress, right? Not really.

The problem with relying on revenue as a measure of progress is that revenue is generally a longer customer life-cycle event, which can mean having to fly blind for a really long time. Mary's team was making huge bets on several big features. Even though her team called them experiments, these were three- to six-month-long initiatives with long build cycles. Her investors had no other option than to accept these product strategies on faith and wait to see what happened.

You need to shorten the feedback loop. Even when revenue is realized, unless you can accurately tie it back to specific actions or events from the past, it is easy to confuse correlation for causality. Mary's teams didn't know what was causing what to happen.

Whenever Mary's company had a good quarter, everyone pointed to their department-level KPIs and took credit. During a bad quarter, the same teams would use the same KPIs to rationalize why the drop in revenue wasn't their fault.

The company's initial momentum began to wear down and growth stagnated. It became increasingly difficult for Mary to justify the return on investment to her stakeholders.

She too found herself spinning the numbers in board meetings. Her go-to measures of progress were either the amount of stuff her team was currently building (build velocity) or the amount of money they made that quarter (booked revenue)—depending on which was better.

Eventually, she too was fired.

> A rising tide lifts all boats, but a falling tide lifts all fingers.

Is There a Way Out?

The mistake Bob made is that he spent a disproportionate amount of time focusing on a fictional business plan that he wasn't able to realize.

Mary had a much better early start, taking a "lean" approach. But despite her best intentions, she found herself drowning in data—and anxiety—as she scaled up her product and team. Her team was looking at the wrong numbers, and these unreliable indicators of progress led them to prioritize the wrong actions, driving her company off course.

To summarize, the traditional measures of progress are unhelpful for the following reasons:

1. Because revenue is near zero during the early stages, we settle for build velocity as a measure of progress. But measuring progress as execution of an untested plan is no better.
2. Investing heavily in quantitative metrics doesn't automatically give you solutions. Metrics can tell you only what's going wrong, not why. The more you invest in quantitative metrics, the more you end up drowning in a sea of nonactionable data.
3. Even when you are generating revenue, unless you can connect cause and effect, you can't leverage the elements that are bringing you success, and you can easily be led down the wrong path.

The *Running Lean* approach, like that of Eric Ries's *Lean Startup*, is grounded in the scientific method and thus sees validated learning as the measure of progress. However, most stakeholders regard business results, not validated learning, as the measure of progress. So we end up building two different stories of our business.

The story we tell our stakeholders is not the same as the story we tell ourselves. They both start out the same but diverge significantly over time because each uses a different definition of progress.

Is there a way out of this dichotomy? That is the promise of this book.

We Need a Single Measure of Progress

The answer lies in first establishing a single metric of progress that both entrepreneurs and stakeholders can reliably use to measure business model success. That metric is traction: the rate at which a business model captures monetizable value from its users. We'll expand upon this definition in chapter 1.

Why isn't the concept of validated learning enough to serve as a workable metric of progress? Validated learning is critical for testing key assumptions and invaluable for keeping our unbridled passion for our products in check. But when this pursuit of learning is carried out at the expense of demonstrable business results, which is often the case, the analogy of "a startup as an experiment" breaks down. We need to realize that the goals of scientists and entrepreneurs are not the same.

Establishing a single measure of progress around traction is key to reconciling the dichotomy of multiple progress stories.

The pursuit of raw knowledge is a scientific pursuit. In that realm, learning is truly the measure of progress. But entrepreneurship is goal driven. Empirical learning is part, but not all, of the final goal: to build a repeatable and scalable business model before running out of resources.

While empirical learning is a key part of that process, unless you can quickly turn that learning into measurable business results, you are just accumulating trivia.

Running Experiments Is Not Enough

Why do so many lean practitioners get stuck running suboptimal experiments? The answer lies in how true science is done. What I learned surprised me:

Running experiments is not considered the most important thing scientists do.

Can you guess what that is?

Albert Einstein was one of the most celebrated scientists of the twentieth century. But he formulated the theory of relativity without running a single empirical experiment. In fact, while Einstein was a student at the Zurich Polytechnic

Institute, he was advised by a professor there to get out of the profession because he wasn't good at devising experiments.

Einstein attributed his breakthrough insights not just to his mathematical and scientific prowess but to his simple mental models. These models were abstracted from the shapes and functions of everyday objects like trains, clocks, and elevators, and they helped him run hundreds of thought experiments. (You might remember some of these from high school physics.)

As I studied other scientists, I found the same repeating pattern:

> Scientists first build a model. Then they use experiments to validate (or invalidate) their model.

Entrepreneurs need models too. *Running Lean* introduced one such model, the Lean Canvas, that can help you deconstruct a complex business idea into a business model. This book introduces two additional complementary models: a traction model and a customer factory model. They will show you how to effectively measure and communicate the output of a working business model.

Waste Is Everywhere

The biggest contributor to suboptimal business results, though, is a lack of focus.

Taiichi Ohno, the father of the Toyota Production System (which later became Lean Manufacturing), is known for drawing a chalk circle on the Toyota factory floor and having managers take turns standing in the circle. Not as punishment, but as an exercise in understanding and seeing waste through deliberate observation.

"Waste is any human activity which absorbs resources but creates no value."

—JAMES P. WOMACK AND DANIEL T. JONES, *LEAN THINKING*

Often a whole shift went by and the manager did not see what Ohno saw, because finding waste in an already efficient factory floor requires experience and effort. Once they began looking in the right places, they might for instance see that a machine operator wastes time walking to the tool room to retrieve a component. This additional step could be eliminated simply by having these components closer at hand.

These types of small improvements, when continually aggregated, yield large results in terms of overall improvement in productivity. However, when applied to innovation, the problem isn't one of finding waste, but rather prioritizing the biggest areas of waste. When operating in an environment riddled with extreme uncertainty and limited resources, it's easy to find waste everywhere. The real challenge is identifying the few key actions that stand to deliver the greatest impact and ignoring the rest.

Think of Ohno's chalk circle exercise as a call to identify your riskiest assumptions. The problem is that uncovering what's riskiest in your business model, while conceptually easy to understand, is hard to put into practice.

"The essence of strategy is choosing what not to do."

—MICHAEL PORTER

Incorrect prioritization of risks is one of the top contributors to waste.

Beyond some obvious initial starting risks like the assumptions you make about who your customers are and what problems they want to solve, risk prioritization requires good intuition and judgment, and it isn't foolproof.

So I went back in search of a better answer, this time to the world of manufacturing.

Your Business Model as a System

One of the most groundbreaking books in the world of manufacturing was undoubtedly *The Goal*, the 1984 business novel by Israeli physicist Eliyahu Goldratt. Through the story of a struggling factory manager, Goldratt introduced the "theory of constraints," a new way of thinking about production systems.

Goldratt makes the case for visualizing the customer value stream *not* as one giant process, but rather as a system of interconnected processes. You can internalize this concept by visualizing the customer value stream as links in a chain.

At any given point in time, one of these links is going to be the weakest link or constraint in the system. If we apply stress to this chain, the entire chain will not fall apart. It will break at its weakest link. Trying to reinforce all the links at once is wasteful because it will not make the chain stronger as a whole. This is the **premature optimization trap**.

In other words, when we're trying to improve any sort of production system, we derive the biggest return on effort only when we correctly identify and focus on the weakest link. What's even more interesting is that as we strengthen this link and reapply stress to this chain, the weakest link moves to a different, and often unpredictable, link in the system.

We can derive two further insights from this. The first is that reinforcing the weakest link will eventually yield zero returns, because another link will eventually take its place as the constraint or the bottleneck, limiting the performance of the entire chain. The second takeaway is that because we cannot predict where the constraint will move, we need to constantly monitor the entire system in search of the next weakest link. Blindly optimizing a single part of the system—even if it was once the weakest link—will eventually lead to waste. This is the **local optimization trap**.

Our business models are no different. At the earliest stages of a business model, the weakest links typically live in your customer and problem assumptions. If those assumptions fall apart, everything else in your business model (your solution, channels, pricing, etc.) also falls apart. Focusing on anything else, like the scalability of your solution, is premature optimization. Beyond the earliest stages, no two products or entrepreneurs are the same. You can't afford to simply guess at what's riskiest. You need a systematic process for uncovering what's riskiest.

The divide-and-conquer approach at Mary's company is a classic example of falling into the local optimization trap. Even though everyone was working tirelessly to optimize their local metrics (local optima), it was at the expense of the overall system throughput (global optima). Her teams should have instead invested effort first toward identifying the weakest link or constraint in their business model, and then collectively focused on solutions for breaking just that constraint.

This book builds upon these concepts and marries systems thinking, *The Lean Startup*, and the scientific method to tackle the innovation challenges I outlined earlier. The next section describes how.

How This Book Is Organized

While *Running Lean* provided a tactical road map for stress testing a business model through experiments, this book goes further. It extends the Lean Canvas business model with additional models and thinking processes that help you make better decisions.

Specifically, it teaches you how to effectively define, measure, and communicate progress with your internal and external stakeholders using the six-step metaframework shown below:

Goal
Observe and Orient
Learn, Leverage, or Lift
Experiment
Analyze
Next Actions

Note the mnemonic GO LEAN, which captures the first letter of each step in this framework. This book is organized into three parts, in chronological order of the steps required to apply this framework.

PART 1: DEFINING PROGRESS

Part 1 makes the case for using traction as the universal measure of progress (**the Goal**). It starts by defining traction and shows you how to turn fuzzy business model goals into a more tangible metric that you can use to ballpark the viability of any business model. Next you'll learn how to break this ballpark goal into more actionable milestones using a traction model.

PART 2: PRIORITIZING WASTE

Part 2 shows you how to benchmark your business model and apply techniques from the theory of constraints to prioritize your riskiest assumptions or constraints in your business model. This is the **Observe and Orient** step in the framework.

PART 3: ACHIEVING BREAKTHROUGH

Part 3 shows you how to use time-boxed LEAN sprints for breaking constraints in your business model. Once a constraint is identified, you formulate a strategy (or Validation Plan) for breaking this constraint by applying the three focusing steps:

1. **Learn** more about the constraint,
2. **Leverage** the constraint, and
3. **Lift** the constraint.

You test these strategies using one or more small, fast, additive **Experiments**. Beyond validated learning, all experiments also need to be tied back to your overall traction model. This is the **Analyze** step from which appropriate **Next Actions** are determined. Together, these make up the **L-E-A-N** steps in the sprint.

How to Use This Book

Each chapter ends with bulleted takeaways that summarize key points. You'll also find exercises along the way that guide you in putting these principles into practice in your own product.

Let's begin.

No methodology can guarantee success. But a good methodology can provide a feedback loop for continual improvement and learning.

PART 1
DEFINING PROGRESS

"If you don't know where you are going,
any road will get you there."

—ADAPTED FROM *ALICE IN WONDERLAND*

Goal
Observe and Orient
Learn, Leverage, or Lift
Experiment
Analyze
Next Actions

CHAPTER 1

Traction Is the Goal

THE FIRST MISTAKE WE MAKE WHEN WE PITCH OUR "GREAT IDEA" TO stakeholders is that we lead with our solution. We spend a disproportionate amount of time talking about the uniqueness of our product's features or its underlying technology breakthroughs. We can't help it—we have the innovator's bias for the solution.

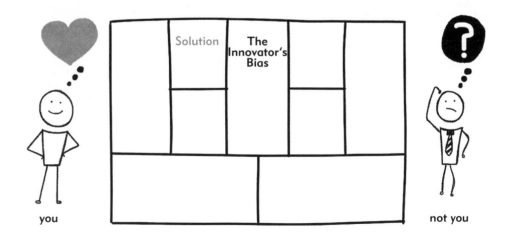

The solution is what we most clearly see and what gets us most excited. But our stakeholders don't necessarily see what we see. More important, their goals are different. They don't care about our solution but rather about a business model story that promises them a return on their investment within a set time frame.

This is what they really want to know:

1. How big is the market opportunity? They don't care who your customers are, but how many—your market size.
2. How will you make money? They want to understand the intersection of your cost structure and revenue streams—your margins.
3. And finally, they want to know how you will defend against copycats and competition that will inevitably enter the market if you are successful—your unfair advantage.

Let's look at an example. Say you have invented a method for reliably capturing an eye-tracking signature. So what? Instead of leading your pitch with a description of your invention, lead with your business model. If this eye-tracking signature can be used as an early diagnostic system for autism in children (big market) at a fraction of the cost of existing alternatives (potential margins), and you have a patent pending on the method (unfair advantage)—*that* is a big deal.

But what gets an investor's attention above everything else is traction. If you walk into an investor's office with the beginnings of a hockey-stick curve, they'll sit you down and try to understand your business model. The hockey-stick curve starts out flat, but has a sharp inflection point when it starts quickly trending up and to the right—indicating that good things are happening.

This inflection point, or evidence of traction, signals that people other than yourself, your team, and possibly your mom care about your idea. The problem is that traction means different things to different people. And it too can be gamed.

It's not enough to simply pick any convenient metric for the y-axis of your

TIME

hockey-stick curve, one that conveniently happens to be going up and to the right, and pass it off as traction. For instance, plotting the cumulative number of users over time has nowhere to go but up and to the right.

A more sophisticated investor will see right through this façade of vanity metrics. You have to instead pick a metric that serves as a reliable indicator for business model growth. In this chapter, I'm going to share such a metric with you.

What Is Traction?

Because traction is a measure of the output of a working business model, let's first turn our attention to the definition of a business model.

> "A business model is a story about how an organization creates, delivers, and captures value."
>
> —SAUL KAPLAN, *THE BUSINESS MODEL INNOVATION FACTORY*

Create Value

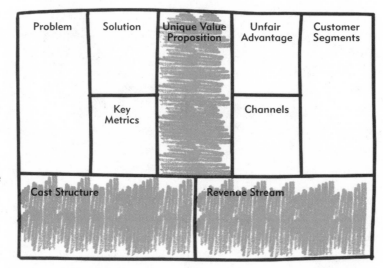

Deliver Value

Capture Value

$

Lean Canvas is adapted from
The Business Model Canvas and
is licensed under the Creative
Commons Attribution-Share
Alike 3.0 Un-ported license.

This business model story can be effectively described using the one-page Lean Canvas tool.

You create value for your customers through your **Unique Value Proposition,** which is the intersection of your customers' problems and your solution. The cost of delivering this value is described by your **Cost Structure**. Some of this value is then captured back through your **Revenue Streams**.

The first insight is that value in the business model is always defined with respect to customers. It follows that the right traction metric must also track a customer action or behavior. Neither the amount of stuff you build, the size of your team, nor your funding qualifies as traction.

The y-axis of your hockey-stick curve needs to measure a customer action.

Next, in order to establish a business model that works, the following two conditions must be met:

1   **Created Value   >   Captured Value**

This is the **value equation** that drives your business model's unique value proposition (UVP). You need to create more value for your customers than you capture back. If your customers don't get back more value (even perceived) than they pay for your product or service, they will not have enough incentive to use your product and your business model will be a nonstarter.

It is equally important that you run tests early in the business model validation process to ensure that you can also capture back some of this value as *monetizable* value that can be converted into revenue. I'm a big proponent of testing this as early in the business model validation process as possible. Otherwise, you delay testing one of the riskiest assumptions in your business model, which can be a costly assumption to get wrong.

Even "free" users in services like Facebook and Twitter aren't truly using these services for free. They pay for their usage through a derivative currency that I'll describe shortly.

2   **Captured Value   >=   Cost (Value Delivery)**

This is the **monetization equation** that drives sustainability and profits in your business model: you need to capture back at least as much value as it costs you to deliver this value or your business model also falls apart.

> There is no business in your business model without revenue.

A for-profit business model aims to maximize the difference between value captured and the cost of delivering value, while a not-for-profit business model aims to keep this difference as close to zero as possible.

$$\text{Created Value} \quad > \quad \text{Captured Value} \quad >= \quad \text{Cost (Value Delivery)}$$

1   **2**

VALUE EQUATION   **MONETIZATION EQUATION**

While every business needs to eventually satisfy both of these equations, it doesn't need to do so from the outset. In the "lean" approach, we tackle them one at a time from left to right. After all, creating value for users is a prerequisite to being able to capture value from them, and capturing value from users is a prerequisite to optimizing your cost structure.

In other words, the value created for customers is an investment in your business model system that is returned when some of that value is converted into revenue.

Capturing value is the common factor in both the value equation and the monetization equation, and key to the definition of traction:

> Traction is the rate at which a business model captures monetizable value from its users.

HOW IS TRACTION DIFFERENT FROM REVENUE?

While booked revenue can be manufactured in many different ways, traction is revenue that needs to be attributable to key user actions in the past. These past user actions serve as leading indicators for extrapolating future business model growth.

I will show you how to deconstruct traction into a set of leading indicators later in the book, but I'll leave you with a simple example for now.

Using customer behavior trends and sales data,* Starbucks realized that time spent in their coffee shops correlated with more money being spent in their stores. In other words, time spent in a coffee shop was a leading indicator of traction. This was a key insight in Starbucks's differentiated positioning of "creating a third space between work and home." While other coffee shops drove you out once you made a purchase, Starbucks welcomed you in, and it paid off very well for them.

The Customer Factory Metaphor

We can make this definition of traction even more tangible by visualizing the output of a working business model as a factory. In this factory metaphor, the job of the factory is to make customers.

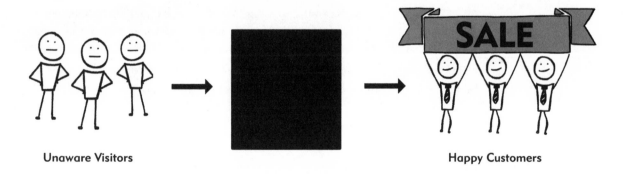

Unaware Visitors **Happy Customers**

---

* Starbucks case study on calculating customer lifetime value: https://blog.kissmetrics.com/how-to-calculate-lifetime-value.

It works by

- taking in unaware visitors as the input on the left,
- creating, delivering, and capturing value from these visitors inside the black box, which we'll deconstruct later, and
- creating happy customers on the right.

Why "happy customers"? Why not "satisfied customers," or just "customers"? The reason I describe the output of this customer factory as "happy customers" is that emotion plays a major role. As you'll see later in the book, the customer factory is *not* simply a mechanical process for cranking out paying customers but rather a well-designed system for making happy customers.

You might also be wondering whether the goal of every business is to create happiness. What about hospitals, insurance companies, and divorce attorneys? I don't believe every business needs to always create smiling customers. But every business does need to create customer value and leave its customers better off than where they started—in other words, to create progress in their customers' journey. So by that definition, even alleviating pain or providing security qualifies as happiness.

Finally, I want to make a subtle but important distinction between making happy customers and making customers happy. Making customers happy is easy. Just give them lots of stuff for free. But that doesn't lead to a working business model. Making happy customers, on the other hand, is not just about making customers feel good but about what they do with your solution. It's about the results.

Kathy Sierra calls this making your customers "badass," a term she landed on after years of experimentation. Other contenders were "passionate" and "awesome." But she settled on "badass" because the other labels implied a goal of making customers *feel* better, as opposed to making them *be* better.

Let's refine our stated business goal of capturing value from users:

> Making happy or badass customers gets you paid. Doing this repeatedly and sustainably is the universal goal of every business.

This is true whether you are building a hardware or software business, a high-tech or no-tech business, or even a for-profit or not-for-profit business. The good news is that we can measure the rate at which we create happy customers using a well-established metric: throughput.

Throughput Is Traction

The customer factory isn't just a cute metaphor. Its reference to manufacturing is intentional. Metaphors are quite powerful when they enable us to transplant and adapt ideas from one domain to another, which is what we are going to do in this book. We can immediately apply one of the key concepts from systems thinking*— the concept of throughput—to further simplify the definition of traction.

Throughput is typically defined as the rate of production or the rate at which items flowing through a system can be processed. In a traditional factory, through-put would measure the rate at which raw materials are turned into finished goods in a specified time interval—for example, 70 units/day.

Measuring throughput this way helps us to see that items in progress (unfin-ished goods or inventory) are a form of waste because they consume resources but don't directly add value. Eliyahu Goldratt has an even stricter definition of through-put. He defines throughput as the rate at which a system generates revenue through

---

* "Systems thinking is the process of understanding how those things which may be regarded as systems influence one another within a complete entity, or larger system" (Wikipedia).

sales. This emphasis on revenue is important because even finished goods sitting in a warehouse take up resources (like storage and electricity) without adding value.

In the customer factory, visitors enter the factory as raw materials, flow through the system as users, and are then processed or converted into customers. Because making customers already implies monetization, we can define traction for a given business model as customer throughput:

> Customer throughput is the rate at which nonpaying users are processed into paying customers.

Under this definition, unless users can be converted into monetizable value (customers), they too are a form of waste. Think of nonpaying users as inventory or investment tied up in your business model that you intend to get back when you turn them into customers.

This definition of customer throughput meets all our earlier criteria for measuring traction: it is customer-centric and it measures the rate at which a business model captures monetizable value from its customers. Because all businesses also have customers, it is universal. Let's put this last statement to the test.

Business Model Archetypes

When people bring up business models, they often use a whole bunch of terms such as software as a service (SaaS), enterprise, retail, e-commerce, ad-based, freemium, viral, social, not-for-profit, marketplace, et cetera.

The reason we end up with dozens of business model descriptors is that we attempt to label the myriad ways that a business model creates, delivers, and captures value. For instance, the difference between SaaS, enterprise, and open-source business models is in how they deliver and capture value. Even within a SaaS business model, one could implement a freemium or trial-based pricing model. Trying to create a list of business model types gets complex pretty fast.

Instead I'm going to take a different approach. We are going to categorize business model types by the number of actors (or customer segments) in the model. Using this approach, we'll define just three basic business model archetypes: direct, multisided, and marketplaces. In the next few sections, I'll show you how to start with these archetypes to describe any type of business.

MODELING DIRECT BUSINESS MODELS

Direct business models are the most basic and widespread type of business model. They are one-actor models where your users become your customers. It's easy to apply the concept of customer throughput to direct business models. A coffee shop is a simple example.

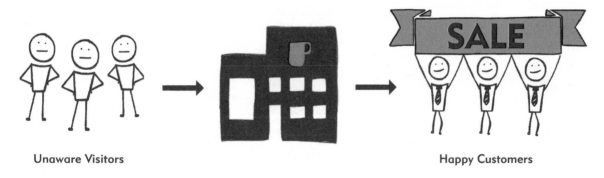

Unaware Visitors   Happy Customers

The coffee shop attracts visitors to its storefront by its ambiance and promise of great drinks. When a visitor, now a user of the coffee shop, purchases a drink, she becomes a customer, and some of this value is captured back as money.

As long as the coffee shop creates more value (even perceived) for its customers than it captures back, the coffee shop creates a happy customer and has a compelling

> Traction in a direct business model is the rate at which you turn nonpaying users into paying customers.

value proposition. And as long as the coffee shop can capture back more value than it costs to deliver this value, it has a sustainable business model.

In a direct business model, monetizable value is extracted directly from your users, who become your paying customers, which is simply the net revenue realized over the life of the customer.

Other examples of one-actor direct business models are:

- Retail
- Software as a service (SaaS)
- Mobile apps
- Physical goods
- Hardware
- Services

WHAT ABOUT THE B2B2C MODEL?

The B2B2C model is one where business A sells its product or service to business B, which is then delivered to the end consumer. This too can be modeled as a direct business model. The key question is determining which customer segment represents the riskier segment, and then modeling every intermediate provider as a channel to reach them.

For example, car companies (with the exception of Tesla Motors) don't sell their vehicles directly to drivers. They use dealers as intermediaries. But because the risk of building the "right car" lies with the drivers, car companies have to model their end customers' needs when designing their vehicles. The dealerships here represent a channel partner that should be listed in the Channel box in the Lean Canvas.

Consider another example: Amazon Web Services. Amazon rents out its datacenters as cloud services that developers buy using a metered usage model. Developers use these services to build all kinds of applications such as games, travel websites, e-commerce sites, et cetera. As long as these developers adhere to Amazon's terms of service, Amazon does not need to understand the details of the end user's needs. Here the developer is the customer.

MODELING MULTISIDED BUSINESSES

The next business model archetype is the multisided business model. Unlike a direct business model where your users become your customers, a multisided business is a multiactor model where your users and customers are different actors (or segments).

In a multisided model, the goal is still to create, deliver, and capture value from users, but that value is monetized through different customers. Users typically don't pay for usage of your product with a monetary currency but with a derivative currency. This derivative currency, when compounded across enough users, represents a derivative asset that your customers pay to acquire.

Let's look at some examples that will make this more concrete:

Ad-Based Business Models

Products like Facebook, Google, Twitter, and YouTube fall under this group of business models. We'll use Facebook as an example. Facebook creates and delivers value to its users through its social network—but doesn't charge its users directly. That said, it still captures some of this value back, albeit through a derivative currency (user attention, in this case).

Facebook then trades this derivative currency on a secondary market of advertisers (its customers), who pay to reach these users.

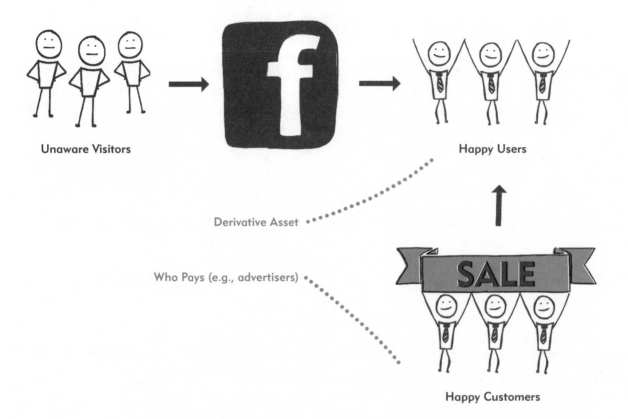

Unaware Visitors

Happy Users

Derivative Asset

Who Pays (e.g., advertisers)

SALE

Happy Customers

We can describe the same business model with Google's search engine business, substituting its search engine for Facebook's social network. In both these examples, the derivative currency is attention, which is monetized by converting attention (from users) into impressions and/or clicks for advertisers (their customers). This conversion of the key monetizable user activity into actual revenue is the derivative currency exchange rate. For ad-based businesses, this is typically described as CPM (cost per thousand impressions), CPC (cost per click), or CPA (cost per acquisition).

Monetizable value, then, is a function of the derivative currency exchange rate, which we can use to calculate the effective monetizable value of users (or an average revenue per user—ARPU) even though they aren't directly paying us. As of Q1 2015, Facebook's annualized advertising ARPU was $9.36.*

Big Data Business Models

Attention isn't the only kind of derivative currency. Another example is data. You might give away a free mobile fitness app to your users and aggregate their usage data into something more valuable that an insurance company, for instance, may want to purchase.

Now for a few not-so-obvious multisided models.

Enterprise

The traditional enterprise product can also be described using the multisided model. Organizations (our customers) are made up of people who play different roles in the business model. There are usually at least two (and sometimes more) roles in the business model.

Users here are the employees who use the product to help the organization realize the value proposition of the product. The customers here are the decision makers who purchase the product for the employees. Some other key roles worth modeling might be the influencers in the organization—for example, the IT department—that have a say in the buy decision.

The basic value flow, however, remains the same. Users of the product create a derivative asset, which, in this case, can be measured as a productivity gain or an improved business process that helps the organization capture more value from its own customers. As long as this asset creates more value to the organization than what the decision makers paid to acquire it, it represents a net positive ROI and a compelling value proposition.

---

* www.statista.com/statistics/430862/facebook-annualized-advertising-arpu/.

Not-for-Profits

Not-for-profits can also be modeled as multisided models. Let's take the Red Cross as an example. The users of the Red Cross are the people in need that the organization serves. And donors are the customers. Because these models are usually impact driven, the number of people helped represents the derivative asset that donors fund. If the Red Cross stopped serving these people, the donations would dry up accordingly.

The common theme across all these business models is that there is a user side and a customer side. The user side is often the riskier of the two sides because that's where monetizable value is created in the form of a derivative asset.

> Traction in a multisided business model is the rate at which you capture monetizable value from your users in the form of a derivative asset.

There are two challenges with derivative assets. The first is that this asset needs to be aggregated over a tipping point of users to make it valuable for customers. For instance, a social network with ten users is not all that interesting to advertisers. The second challenge is that the derivative currency exchange rate (how much an advertiser would pay in this example), like any derivative asset, is not a given, and fluctuates over time. For these reasons, an effective validation strategy is to first tackle the user side of the model until a sufficient tipping point is achieved.

The key in multisided models is establishing the derivative currency exchange rate early. This helps demonstrate the business model story, which drives valuation of the business. The more liquid this conversion, the higher the valuation. This is exactly why Facebook commands a higher valuation per active users than Twitter, which commands a higher valuation than Snapchat.

The next business model archetype is a special case of the multisided model.

MODELING MARKETPLACES

Marketplace models are a more complex variant of the multisided model that warrant their own category. Like multisided models, marketplaces are multiactor models made up of two different segments: buyers and sellers. eBay, AngelList, and Airbnb are all examples of marketplace business models. But unlike the multisided model where users are the riskier side and can be tackled serially before customers, in a marketplace model both the buyer and seller sides need to be tackled simultaneously.

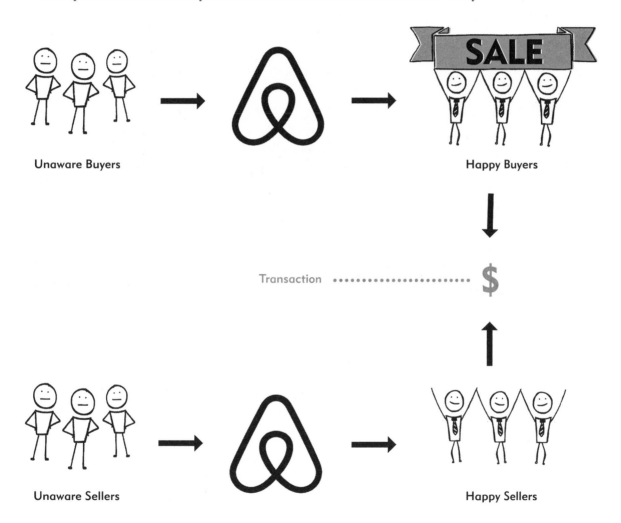

Sure, some marketplaces will naturally be buyer-led while others will be seller-led, allowing you to start building out one side before the other. But ultimately you need to bring both sides together *simultaneously* to conduct a transaction. The transaction is the key activity that creates happy customers.

Monetizable value in these models is typically captured as a percentage of the value of the transaction created between buyer and seller as a commission, listing fee, et cetera.

The reason this is the most complex business model archetype is that you have two customer factories that need to be firing together. A key pattern for success with this model is first identifying a preexisting marketplace with lots of transactional friction. If you can remove some of this friction for your early-adopter buyers and sellers, you represent a compelling value proposition that draws buyers and sellers from their existing alternative(s) to your marketplace.

> Traction in a marketplace model is NOT the rate at which you create buyers or sellers (listings), but the rate at which you bring both sides together to conduct a transaction.

- eBay did this for the collectibles marketplace, where the existing alternatives were garage sales and antique shops.
- AngelList did this for the startup funding marketplace, where the existing alternative was hitting the pitching circuit.
- Airbnb did this for the rooms marketplace, where the existing alternatives were hotel rooms and couch surfing.

Not All Customers Are Created Equal

Even though making customers automatically implies monetization, not all customers are created equal. Would you rather create 100 customers/year or 1,000 customers/year? What if you kept both customer segments for a year and the first customer segment generated an average lifetime value of $100 while the second customer segment generated an average lifetime value of $5?

> Lifetime Value (LTV) is the projected revenue that a customer will generate during his lifetime.

CUSTOMER SEGMENT	A	B
Number of Customers	100	1,000
LTV per Customer	$100	$5
Total LTV	$10,000	$5,000

Before you rush to declare customer segment A the more valuable group, don't forget to factor in the cost of raw materials or the Cost of Customer Acquisition (COCA).

If the first group was acquired through an expensive paid channel or sales process, while the second group was acquired through a cheaper organic channel, the right answer could be reversed.

> Cost of Customer Acquisition (COCA) is the cost of getting a potential customer to buy your product.

Throughput, then, is NOT simply the rate at which you create customers (measured as customer throughput), but the net monetizable value captured from them in a given period.

That said, measuring customer throughput (people) is more tangible and actionable than measuring throughput (revenue). For this reason, we will often convert throughput into customer throughput in this book.

Let's consider a final scenario: assuming similar cost of customer acquisition and customer lifetimes, what if the first customer segment of 100 customers generated a $100 LTV while the second customer segment of 1,000 customers generated a $10 LTV? Which is the more valuable group of customers? Warning: this is also a trick question.

CUSTOMER SEGMENT	A	B
Number of Customers	100	1,000
LTV per Customer	$100	$10
Total LTV	$10,000	$10,000

Even though both customer segments appear to generate the same throughput, throughput is *not* profit. Once we factor in operating expenses to service these customers, the net profit across both groups may no longer be the same. It may work out better to have fewer high-margin customers than lots of low-margin customers. But the opposite may also be true, depending on the relative costs to service each of these customer segments.

The point of these exercises is to highlight that you'll often have a choice of what type of customer to make or what customer segment to pursue. Each potential customer segment will have a different customer acquisition (raw material) cost and will use up a different amount of operating expenses for converting users into customers. These differences should be weighed against one another carefully when considering your business model variants.

A Brief Primer on Throughput Accounting

Goldratt uses three metrics—throughput, inventory, and operating expenses—as the basis for a new accounting paradigm he described as "throughput accounting." In contrast to the more traditional cost-based accounting paradigm, throughput accounting prioritizes value creation over cost cutting.

Let's first more formally define each metric as it maps to the customer factory:

1. Throughput

    Throughput is the rate at which monetizable value is generated from your customers over their lifetime minus any totally variable costs such as the cost of raw materials—typically the cost of customer acquisition.

2. Inventory

    Inventory represents all the money invested in the customer factory toward things it intends to sell. This includes things you expect, like your product, but also unfinished goods (users), finished goods (customers), equipment, and other infrastructure that goes into the manufacturing of these goods (e.g., servers, software, etc.). The term "inventory" is interchangeable with "investment" in your system.

3. Operating Expenses

    Operating expenses are the costs expended turning inventory into throughput. They include things like salaries and other costs incurred in the running of the system. The distinction between inventory and operating expenses may appear fuzzy. It helps to think of inventory as assets that contribute to the valuation of a company and everything else as an operating expense.

The picture on the next page summarizes the relationship between these three metrics:

We can use these three metrics to calculate profit as:

$$P = T - OE$$

where

P = Profit
T = Total Throughput
OE = Operating Expenses

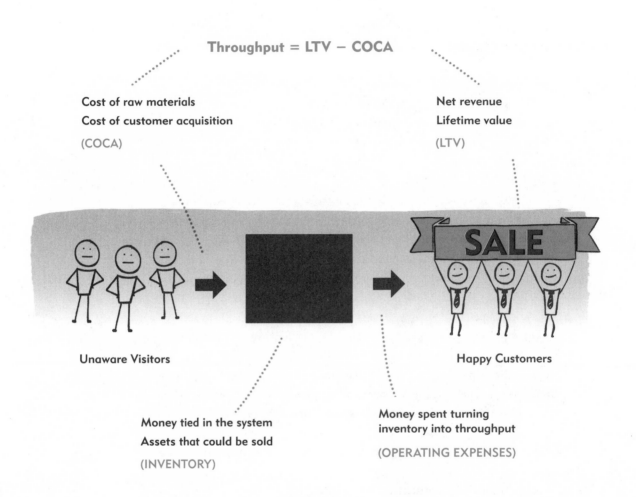

Throughput = LTV − COCA

Cost of raw materials
Cost of customer acquisition
(COCA)

Net revenue
Lifetime value
(LTV)

SALE

Unaware Visitors

Happy Customers

Money tied in the system
Assets that could be sold
(INVENTORY)

Money spent turning
inventory into throughput
(OPERATING EXPENSES)

Cost-based accounting places more emphasis on the right-hand side of the profit equation—decrease operating expenses. It focuses on scalable efficiency and squeezing out costs—especially labor costs. This typically manifests itself as policies requiring detailed weekly time sheets broken down by task, as well as downsizing, outsourcing, and other cost-reducing measures.

It is much more powerful to try to affect the left-hand side of the profit equation—increase throughput—because cost cutting has a theoretical limit of zero. Increasing throughput has no theoretical upper limit. You can find ways to add more value to an existing product, build more add-on products, or expand the market—provided, of course, that these efforts lead to a positive return on investment:

$$ROI = (T - OE) / I$$

where

ROI = Return on Investment
T = Total Throughput
OE = Operating Expenses
I = Inventory

You can see that a decrease in inventory (or the investment in the system) increases ROI. While decreasing inventory ranks higher than decreasing operating expenses, it still takes a backseat to increasing throughput because decreasing inventory also has a theoretical limit of zero.

Increasing throughput is the only macro that matters.

This interrelationship between throughput, inventory, and operating expenses is what Goldratt describes as the goal:

> The universal goal of every business is to increase throughput while minimizing inventory and operating expenses provided doing that doesn't degrade throughput.

This is a more nuanced goal than simply aiming for "increasing traction." You might for instance be able to increase throughput (traction) by selling to a new customer segment. But before deciding to move forward, you should take both the increase in inventory and possible increase in operating expenses into account. Simply focusing on one metric in isolation does not guarantee the desired outcome.

The picture below depicts the universal goal along with some typical line items you'd find under each category.

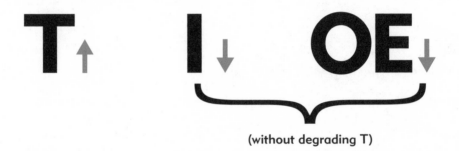

(without degrading T)

Revenue	Users and Customers	Product Development
Derivative Currencies	Features/Product	Customer Service
	Equipment/Infrastructure	Marketing
		Hosting Costs
		Software Subscriptions

Before moving forward, trying ad-libbing the goal using each of these items and see if it makes sense to you.

Examples:

1. The goal is to increase *monetizable value* while minimizing the number of *users* and *customer service* costs.

2. The goal is to increase *monetizable value* while minimizing the number of *features* and *product development* costs.

3. The goal is to increase *monetizable value* while minimizing the number of *servers* and *hosting* costs.

Increasing throughput while minimizing inventory and operating expenses is the ideal, but of course, not always possible. Growth requires an investment in inventory (e.g., adding more users and features), which will often also result in an increase in operating expenses (e.g., hiring more people). But as long as your decision results in a net positive ROI over time, you move closer to the goal.

Exercise: Describe Your Business Model Story

Now it's your turn.

1. Go to http://LeanStack.com and create a free account.
2. Describe your business model(s) using the Lean Canvas tool.
3. Categorize your business model into one of the three business model archetypes: direct, multisided, or marketplace. While it's tempting to simultaneously layer more than one business model type with your idea, it's better to keep your starting models simple. Remember that every complex system first starts out as a simple system. If your idea can be potentially realized using multiple business model types, create a separate Lean Canvas for each variant.
4. Then identify the key monetizable activity in your business model. A revenue story is the key differentiator between a business model and a hobby.
5. Next place a value (either a direct or derivative value) on this key activity.

Business Model Search Versus Execution

With your first business model created, it's time to consider variants. Just as rushing to build a solution can lead to waste, so can limiting yourself to a single business model. Prematurely narrowing down may lead to a suboptimal business model because, at the outset, your business model possibilities are numerous and you don't yet know what you don't know. For these reasons I describe the entrepreneurial journey in *Running Lean* as a search-versus-execution problem—best visualized using the hill climbing (or local maximum) problem from computer science.

Here's the scenario: Imagine you were parachuted blindfolded onto the land-

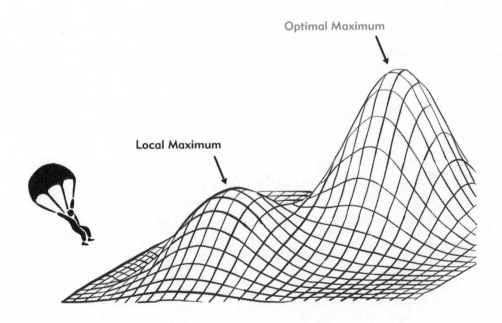

Optimal Maximum

Local Maximum

scape opposite and tasked with finding the highest point. Fumbling around, you might be able to make your way to the top of the hill (the local maximum) but miss the neighboring mountain right next to you because your field of vision was limited. You are prone to this same local maximum trap when searching for a business model.

While there is no foolproof way of completely avoiding this trap, you raise your odds of avoiding a local maximum when you initially open yourself to exploring and even testing multiple business models in parallel.

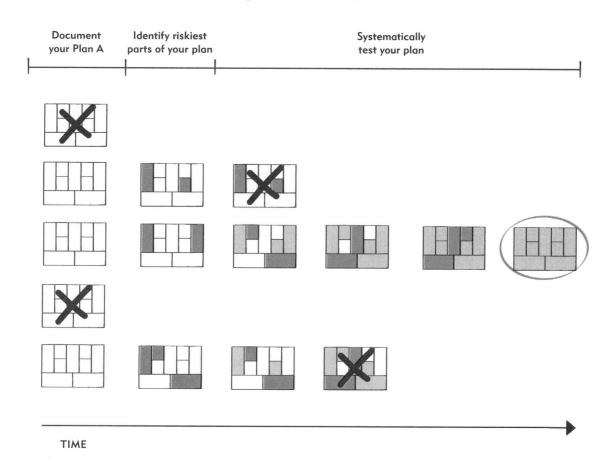

Exercise: Create Business Model Variants

Revisit your business model and create a few variants. Here are some possible variables to tweak:

- Customer segments: Are there other types of customers who share similar problems and thus represent a different business model?
- Problem positioning: Does leading with a different set of problems result in a different business model?
- Pricing model: Does changing how you capture back monetizable value change your business model?

Key Takeaways

- Traction is the one metric that matters above everything else.
- Traction is the rate at which a business model captures monetizable value from its users.
- For a given business model, the rate at which you create customers (customer throughput) is traction.
- There are three business model archetypes: direct, multisided, and marketplace models.
- A direct business model is a one-actor model where users become your customers.
- A multisided model is made up of users who generate a derivative asset that customers buy.
- A marketplace model is made up of buyers and sellers who come together to conduct a transaction.

CHAPTER 2

The Back-of-the-Envelope Business Model Test

NOW THAT WE HAVE A UNIVERSAL METRIC FOR DESCRIBING THE OUTPUT of a business model, let's turn our attention back to an even earlier problem: demonstrating the "potential of an idea." You'll have to justify your new venture to a VC, CFO, spouse, or even yourself as a prerequisite to securing runway. In this chapter, you'll learn to quickly estimate the viability of a new business model without needing to create an overly elaborate financial forecast.

The mistake we make with financial projections at the business planning phase is that we spend a disproportionate amount of time focusing on the output of our models when it's the inputs that really matter. In this chapter, I'll show you how to quickly ballpark a business model and test its viability using a simple back-of-the-envelope calculation.

Meet Enrico Fermi

Enrico Fermi was an Italian physicist who was famous for making rapid order-of-magnitude estimations with seemingly little available data.

Fermi worked on the Manhattan Project, developing the atomic bomb. When it was tested at the Trinity site in 1945, Fermi wanted a rough estimate of the blast's power before the actual data came in. He dropped a few pieces of paper during the blast and used the distance they traveled as they fell to estimate the strength of the explosion. His estimate of 10 kilotons of TNT was remarkably close to the actual value of 18.6 kilotons of TNT given the data he had.

If you've ever tried to estimate how many pieces of candy there are in a jar, you've been exposed to a Fermi problem. Fermi estimates, or back-of-the-envelope calculations, work by making justified guesses to a problem's input assumptions that are accurate within an order of magnitude (the nearest power of ten). This is often the best we can do with little data, but it's surprising how useful this kind of ballpark estimate can be in making a decision.

To illustrate this, let me demonstrate the process using another classic example of a Fermi problem.

How Many Piano Tuners Are There in Chicago?

When confronted with a question like this, most people shy away from giving any answer because the level of uncertainty is paralyzing. But let's break this down into a set of input assumptions.

1. How many people live in Chicago?

    We aren't aiming for a precise answer here, but rather a ballpark estimate that needs to be accurate only within an order of magnitude (power of ten).

    Would you say the population of Chicago is 100,000, 1,000,000, or 10,000,000? We know Chicago is a big city, but not enormous. So it can't be 10 million. We'll go with 1 million people.

    Note: It is okay to look up easily accessible input values like this one. But for this exercise we'll stick with power-of-ten estimates.

2. How many pianos are in Chicago?

Now that we have an estimate for the population, let's estimate how many pianos there are. Which do you think is a reasonable estimate:

1 out of every 10 people has a piano.

1 out of every 100 people has a piano.

1 out of every 1000 people has a piano.

This is our second power-of-ten estimation step. Remember, we need to account for families and children. We'll go with the middle answer: 1 out of every 100 people in Chicago has a piano. So that would put the number of pianos in Chicago at $(1,000,000 \times 0.01) = 10,000$ pianos.

3. How many pianos can a piano tuner tune in a year?

We're now going to tie the number of pianos to piano tuners with our third (and final) estimation step.

This is a harder estimation than the previous ones. You can formulate a bunch of additional input assumptions, such as how long it might take a piano tuner to tune one piano and how long it might take him to travel between pianos, to come up with an estimate of how many pianos he can tune in a day. You could then multiply this number by the number of working days in a year to get the number of pianos a piano tuner tunes in a year.

That is a reasonable approach, but we don't even need to go through all that work to make a quick estimate. We can again ballpark this using a power-of-ten estimate. Would you say a piano tuner typically tunes 10, 100, or 1,000 pianos a year? To be able to tune 1,000 pianos a year, he would have to tune close to 4 pianos every day (not counting weekends)—which seems unrealistic. So let's go with 100 pianos a year.

How Many Piano Tuners Are There in Chicago?

Coming up with an answer to our original question is now simple math:

$$\text{Number of Piano Tuners} = \frac{\text{10,000 Pianos}}{\text{100 Pianos Tuned in a Year}}$$

$$= \text{100 Piano Tuners}$$

How do we feel about this number? We can check our answer against the Chicago Yellow Pages (phone book), which reveals 81 piano tuners!

No, this wasn't a magic trick. The reason Fermi estimates work is that the overestimates and underestimates balance each other out and produce an estimation that is usually within one order of magnitude of the actual answer.

Estimating business models is no different. In the next section, we'll put our newly acquired traction metric of throughput and the Fermi estimation method to use.

How to Test Whether a Business Model Is Worth Pursuing

Before you can test whether a specific business model is worth pursuing, you first need to ballpark the finished story benefit—or desired outcome—which is orthogonal to your business model.

I know this sounds a lot like the "exit number" question investors ask, and I can already sense your uneasiness. Most people hate this question because it feels like arbitrarily picking yet another large number out of thin air (like a $100M exit goal) and then working Excel magic to rationalize the number.

But this number isn't quite pulled out of thin air. Even a $100M exit number has a rationale behind it. VC firms take active board member positions in the companies they invest in, which immediately limits their portfolio size to about ten companies. Given that nine out of ten startups fail, this constraint forces them to seek only companies that are aiming big enough in order to make their own business model work. Hence the need for the $100M exit story.

This number doesn't have to be $100M, of course. The "right" number is a function of your business model incubation environment.

If instead of a high-growth startup you were exploring a new business model in an enterprise setting, there would similarly need to be some discussion of an expected return (one with a lot of zeros too) to justify the effort expended.

Even as a solo bootstrapper, you probably have (and if not, should have) some ballpark number to justify your return on effort per project. This could very well be a $100M exit, but could just as well also be generating an extra $1,000/month of passive income.

There is no right or wrong answer, but you should have an answer. We need this number to justify our business model story—first to ourselves and then to our internal and external stakeholders (team, investors, budget gatekeepers, etc.). I'll warn you that this can be a deep (and often uncomfortable) thought exercise that gets to your personal "why," but the constraints it exposes allow for a more actionable strategy.

USERcycle Case Study

The backstory of this product was that I stumbled into a potential opportunity for productizing a homegrown solution I had originally built for myself. While running workshops, I related my challenge of making sense of

"Business is a means to an end. Do a life plan before you make your business plans."

—NORM BRODSKY AND BO BURLINGHAM, *THE KNACK*

> Your business model, NOT your solution, is the product.

quantitative metrics and offered some solutions that resonated with people in the room who approached me afterward. A few years ago, I would have taken this anecdotal "customer pull" for a solution as enough to justify going down the productization path, but having done this one too many times before, I decided to first test whether I could describe an underlying business model with a problem worth solving.

My next step was sketching a one-page business model using a Lean Canvas worksheet:

PROBLEM	SOLUTION	UNIQUE VALUE PROPOSITION	SOLUTION	CUSTOMER SEGMENTS
1. Hard to measure real progress	1. Companywide dashboard	Not more numbers but actionable metrics	1. Personal authority	Software companies
2. Drown in sea of numbers	2. Measure only 5 macro metrics		2. Respected domain expert advisers	
3. Metrics can't tell you why	3. Life-cycle messaging			

EXISTING ALTERNATIVES	KEY METRICS	HIGH LEVEL CONCEPT	CHANNELS	EARLY ADOPTERS
1. Homegrown	1. Number of trials	KISSmetrics meets MailChimp	Blog	SaaS products
2. Analytics and CRM software	2. Upgrades to paying accounts		Workshops	
	3. Lifetime value		Content marketing	
			Facebook/Google ads	

COST STRUCTURE	REVENUE STREAMS
1 developer, 1 designer, 1 marketer	SaaS model: $50/mo
Server (free hosting)	

Lean Canvas is adapted from The Business Model Canvas (www.businessmodelgeneration.com) and is licensed under the Creative Commons Attribution-Share Alike 3.0 Un-ported License.

Here is what my business model story sounded like:

When software companies first launch a product, lots of things can and do go wrong. The common tendency is to want to collect as much data as possible, but instead of getting clarity, they end up drowning in a sea of data. Metrics were supposed to be the answer, but they tell you only what's going wrong—not why or how to fix it.

Our solution is to provide a companywide dashboard made up of just five macro metrics that help software teams measure progress without drowning in a sea of data. More important, they can get to the users behind the numbers and automate life-cycle e-mail messages to their users based on the actions they take or don't take in the product. This allows software teams to close their learning loop and get to the reasons for the good or bad metrics. The high-level concept of this idea is: KISSmetrics meets MailChimp.

While this problem/solution combo can be applied in a wide array of software companies, we have identified our early adopters as a subset of software companies that offer their software as a recurring service. Our team has the most firsthand experience with these types of products, and our unique value proposition can be demonstrated quickly there.

We stumbled into this business model through workshops which represent a good starting channel that also plays into our unfair advantage. We would scale our channels by investing more heavily in content marketing—possibly offering an Actionable Metrics workshop and other related content.

Most software founders typically spend $0 (Google Analytics) to ~$100/month (other third-party analytics products). Based on this, we will offer a starting price of $50/month.

What do you think? Given this business model story, does it represent a business model worth pursuing? While the Lean Canvas tool allows you to quickly capture your business model story, it's hard to answer this question without digging into some more numbers.

The traditional top-down approach for doing this is attaching your business model to a "large enough" customer segment. Then the logic goes that if you can capture "just 1 percent" of this large market, you'll be all set. After all, 1 percent of a billion-dollar market is still a lot of zeros....

The problems with this approach are that:

- it gives you a false sense of comfort,
- it doesn't address how to get to this 1 percent market share with your specific product, and, finally,
- 1 percent market share might not even be the right success criteria for you.

There is a much better bottom-up approach. Here are the steps:

1. Determine Your Minimum Success Criteria

Instead of thinking in terms of your business model's maximum upside potential (like the 1 percent market share goal), it's more helpful to think in terms of time-boxed minimum success criteria.

Your minimum success criteria are the smallest outcomes that would deem the project a success for you X years from now.

If, for instance, you had asked the Google or Facebook founders when they were first starting out whether they thought they would go on to build billion-dollar companies, they would probably have laughed at you.

This is what Mark Zuckerberg said in an interview about the early days of Facebook:

> "We built it and we didn't expect it to be a company, we were just building this because we thought it was awesome."
>
> —MARK ZUCKERBERG

That said, after Facebook's first year of operations it was offered a $50M acquisition by Myspace. Zuckerberg countered with $75M, which Myspace turned down. While Mark Zuckerberg might still not have been able to predict building a billion-dollar business at that time, he did have a number in mind at the one-year point.

In the case of Google, we know that despite building a very successful search engine, Larry Page and Sergey Brin struggled for years to find a sustainable business model. Out of desperation, they even tried to get themselves acquired by Yahoo for $1M, which got turned down. So at that point in time, we could say that their minimum success criteria morphed from whatever they started at to $1M. That didn't keep the Google founders from going on to build a billion-dollar company.

And that's the point. No one ever penalizes you for revising your goal upward. But if you don't have a reasonable minimum goal, it's hard to define what success will look like. Not only are the minimum success criteria easier to estimate than your maximum upside potential, they also help you model your progress along the way.

Here are some guidelines for defining your minimum success criteria:

1. Keep your time box under three years.

    Anything longer becomes too far to see. The key is picking a date just far enough into the future that it allows you to demonstrate a working version of your business model.

2. Frame the outcome in terms of a revenue (or throughput) goal.

    A yearly revenue goal more directly maps to the revenue streams listed on your Lean Canvas and keeps the model simple. Profit and valuation are derivations of revenue anyway, and here's how to incorporate them.

If you'd like to target a profit goal, use a gross margin assumption to convert your profit goal into a revenue goal. For instance, healthy SaaS products typically target a gross margin above 80 percent.

If you'd like to target a valuation goal instead, use a valuation multiple like a price/sales ratio to convert your valuation target to a revenue target. As these valuations are highly dependent on market conditions, your best bet is researching valuation multiples of recent companies that have raised funding or been acquired.

3. Remember that the goal is a rough ballpark.

You are not looking for three-digit precision here, but an initial estimate that is accurate only within an order of magnitude. In other words, first ask yourself whether you are aiming to build a $100K/year, $1M/year, $10M/year, or $100M/year business. You can then narrow a bit further from there.

My minimum success criteria for the SaaS product I was considering were $10M/year in revenue within three years. While this throughput number makes my goal more concrete, it is still just a fuzzy revenue number and still decoupled from the actual specifics in my business model. The next step is converting this throughput number into a customer throughput number.

2. Convert Your Minimum Success Criteria to Customer Throughput

In order to calculate the customer throughput needed, the first critical input we need is a pricing model. I review lots of Lean Canvases where this isn't specified.

Even at the early ideation stage, you need to get specific on pricing. The biggest objection I often hear is: "How can I price a product when my solution is still uncertain?"

Price against their problems (using value-based pricing) and not what it's going to cost you to build and deliver your solution (that's a cost structure concern). You do this by anchoring against their existing alternatives, which should ideally provide evidence of monetizable pain.

Again, precision here is not the goal but an estimate. First estimate to an order of magnitude. Is your solution potentially worth $1/month, $10/month, $100/month, $1,000/month, $10,000/month? Then use your knowledge of your customers' existing alternatives to get more specific. That is how I estimated my $50/month starting price point.

Customers care about their problems, not your solution.

The best evidence of monetizable pain is a check being written.

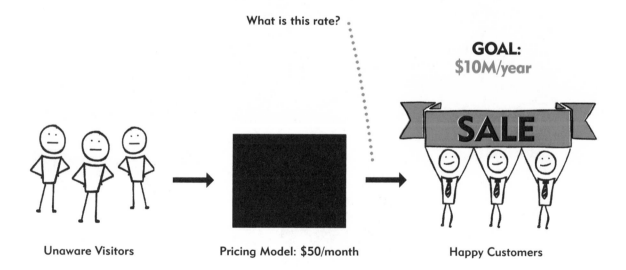

What is this rate?

GOAL:
$10M/year

SALE

Unaware Visitors   Pricing Model: $50/month   Happy Customers

At this point, it's simple to figure out the number of active customers I would need to sustain my business model objective:

$$\text{Number of Active Customers} = \frac{\text{Yearly Revenue Target}}{\text{Yearly Customer Revenue}}$$

$$= \text{\$10M} / (\text{\$50/month} \times 12 \text{ months})$$

$$= \text{16,000+ Active Customers}$$

This is already a better number than the fuzzy $10M revenue goal because it makes the number more tangible. You can immediately test this number against your customer segment to ensure that it's big enough.

While a number of active users is better than just a revenue goal, it still reveals only a part of the story. The danger of relying only on this number is that it's easy to believe that all we need to do is reach this number of active customers one time and

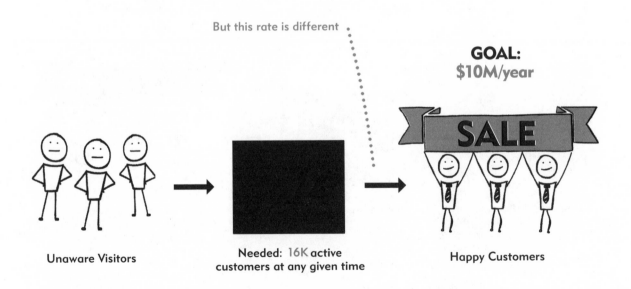

But this rate is different

GOAL:
$10M/year

SALE

Unaware Visitors

Needed: 16K active customers at any given time

Happy Customers

we're set. But it does not factor in customer attrition or churn. Customers leave as a natural part of every business.

Another way of stating this is that the number of active customers represents the steady state number of customers that you need to maintain to sustain your throughput goal, but it's *not* a measure of the rate at which you need to create new customers to replace those who leave.

To get this rate, we need to first estimate a customer's potential lifetime, from which we can calculate their lifetime value.

ESTIMATING LTV

Here are some ways to tackle estimating a typical customer lifetime:

1. Does your value proposition have recurring utility?

   One way to guess at the customer lifetime is through the nature of the problem you are solving. Is it a single-occurrence problem or something recurring? If recurring, how frequently would users need to solve the problem and for how long? From there you might be able to guess when they might outgrow your solution.

2. Think in terms of jobs.

   Clayton Christensen first popularized the jobs-to-be-done concept in his book *The Innovator's Solution*. The basic premise is that customers hire your product or service to get a certain job done.

   Once this job is done, your customers move on—not because they hate your product, but quite the opposite. If you hire a painter to paint your house, you expect him to be done in a few days. If he is still there two months later, that's probably a bad sign. Once you can clearly articulate the job your customers hire your product to do, it becomes easier to estimate the average time it might take to accomplish the job.

In my example, my target early adopters are early-stage software companies. Statistically, about half of new products fail within their first three years. This gives me a ballpark customer lifetime to use.

3. Study other analogs.

Studying other analogs in your vertical, or domain, can also be an effective way of estimating your average customer lifetime. In the SaaS world, for instance, Salesforce (the largest company in this space) reports a four-year customer lifetime. It doesn't mean you can't do better, but it helps to ground your own estimates.

These numbers can usually be found online with just a little research. Successful companies frequently report their numbers publicly on analyst calls, to reporters, or even on their own blogs and other PR channels.

4. If you're still stuck . . .

If all else fails, pick a conservative estimate for now. For this exercise, you need smaller gradations than powers of ten. If you're aiming for more than ten years, you're either in a business with lots of customer lock-in or off by a lot. A more conservative estimate for most business models is somewhere between less than a year (a one-time-use product) and five years. In my example, I decided to use a two-year customer lifetime as a conservative estimate.*

Once you have a projected customer lifetime and pricing model, go ahead and calculate your projected LTV. For this business model, we can then calculate the required customer throughput rate as:

---

* This was based on the statistic that most startups (my early adopter target) fail within three years (source: Startup Genome).

Yearly Revenue Target	=	$10M/year revenue
Customer Lifetime Value (LTV)	=	$50/month for 2 years life term
	=	$1,200 LTV

$$\text{Customer Throughput Rate} = \frac{\text{Yearly Revenue Target}}{\text{Customer Lifetime Value}}$$

	=	$10M/$1,200 LTV
	=	8,333 new customers/year

Make sure you work the numbers out for yourself before moving on. People usually have no problem calculating the number of active customers needed for $10M/year revenue, which we previously calculated as 16,000-plus active customers. But the 8,000-plus new customers/year isn't the number of active customers, but rather the number of new customers you need to make every year after you hit your minimum success criteria—just to sustain your desired throughput.

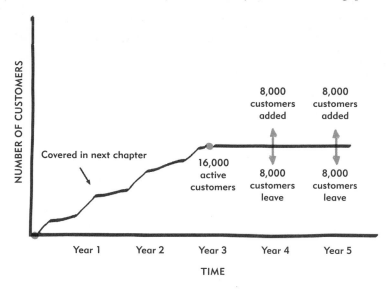

The point of this exercise is getting a first dose of reality on the viability of your business model. What do you think about the viability of this business model now? Creating 16,000 active customers one time is very different from having to create 8,000 new customers every year just to maintain your desired revenue goal!

3. Test/Refine Your Business Model Against Your Minimum Success Criteria

The purpose of this simple back-of-the-envelope calculation is to turn a big fuzzy revenue number into something real and tangible—like creating customers.

| All metrics are people first.

It's much easier to do a gut test with people than with just numbers: "How does having to add 8,000-plus new SaaS customers every year make you feel?" I aim to achieve my minimum success criteria goal using just my early adopter segment (which is a smaller segment of the overall customer segment) to give myself room for further growth. A quick lookup reveals that there are about 10,000 active SaaS products today, which signals a red flag on the viability of this business model.

It gets worse. Most SaaS products average a 1 percent conversion rate from visitors to customers. So in order to generate 8,000-plus new customers, I would need to drive 800,000-plus new visitors per year. That's 2,000-plus new visitors per day!

Once you have these customer throughput rates, you can then revisit your Lean Canvas and put your customer segment and channel assumptions to the test.

- Is your customer segment big enough?
- Do you have any scalable channels identified already for building a reliable enough path to customers?

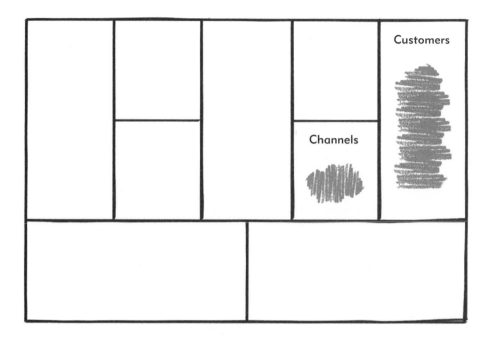

In my case, while the overall software market might be large enough to sustain these numbers, I wasn't confident I could do this with just my SaaS early adopter segment. So I decided to refine my business model further. The levers for driving down the customer production rate are obvious from the formula:

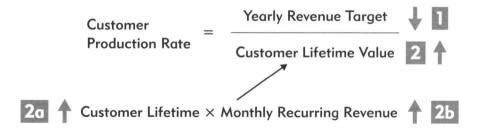

1. Lower Yearly Revenue Target

    You can always lower your yearly revenue target, but because that requires us to lower our desired outcome, we'll leave this option as a last resort.

2. Increase Customer Lifetime Value

    The only other option is increasing your customer lifetime value. In this example, customer lifetime value is a function of the customer lifetime and the monthly recurring revenue (MRR). Let's look at each in turn:

    a. Increase your customer life term

    Doubling our customer life term from two years to four years would halve our customer production rate requirement. That said, increasing customer lifetime is nontrivial because it potentially requires a revamp to the existing value proposition, and possibly the scope of the solution, which drives up product delivery costs (or operating expenses).

    b. Raise pricing

    This is by far the most powerful (and underutilized) lever you have in your business model. Doubling pricing from $50/month to $100/month also cuts the required customer production rate in half. But unlike increasing the utility of your value proposition, a price change may take only a few minutes to implement on your checkout page.

Sure, there is always the danger that increasing pricing will result in fewer customers, but what if it doesn't? Consider Joe's story. I met Joe six months after he had launched his product. He was charging $30/month at the time and making a few thousand dollars a month. While he was happy he was making some money, he felt stuck because he wasn't making enough money to invest in growth. I immediately challenged his pricing assumptions. Like many entrepreneurs, Joe had made the mistake of using a cost-based pricing approach.

Cost-based pricing is where you estimate what it costs you to deliver your product and then slap a modest margin on top of that. This approach usually leaves uncaptured value (money) on the table. I asked Joe to think about raising prices this way:

> If you could double your pricing, and not lose more than half your customers, you would still come out ahead.

You come out ahead because you keep the same throughput but now have fewer customers. Fewer customers (less inventory) mean fewer customer support requests and lower operating costs to service them.

I managed to convince him by pointing out that he could limit the new pricing test just to new customers and run the test for only two weeks. I met with him two weeks later and he was ecstatic. He had signed up the same number of customers as he had the previous two weeks—only at twice the price! I asked him what he was going to do next. He shot back: "I'm going to double my pricing again!"

He doubled his pricing and while he measured a slight dip, he was still far away from the threshold, so he decided to double his pricing another time. This time he did measure a significant dip and settled on a price that was four times higher than where he had started.

Joe's story is not atypical. Most entrepreneurs price their products like artists. They struggle to place a fair value on their product and fall back on a cost-based pricing approach like Joe did. A more effective approach is thinking in terms of value-based pricing in which you anchor your pricing not against your cost structure but against the potential value your customers stand to derive from your product. Remember that as long as your customers derive more value from your product than it costs them, it's still a fair transaction.

Like Joe, I didn't choose to simply double my pricing, I chose to quadruple it to $200/month. Here's how the rest of the numbers worked out:

Yearly Revenue Target	=	**$10M/year revenue**
Customer Lifetime Value (LTV)	=	**$200/month for 2 years life term**
	=	**$4,800 LTV**

$$\text{Customer Throughput Rate} = \frac{\text{Yearly Revenue Target}}{\text{Customer Lifetime Value}}$$

$$= \$10\text{M}/\$4{,}800 \text{ LTV}$$

$$= 2{,}083 \text{ new customers/year}$$

Isn't This All Just Funny Math?

At this point, you might be wondering whether all this is even worth the trouble. After all, you can easily double or quadruple the pricing model on paper to make the model work. So what?

> While we all need a ballpark destination to justify the journey, it's not the destination itself but the starting assumptions that inform whether we are even on the right path.

We started with a big fuzzy revenue goal (the destination) and first converted it into a customer throughput rate. We then further deconstructed this number into a set of input parameters (starting assumptions). Some of these starting assumptions can actually be validated on day one.

While quadrupling your price (like I did) is easy on paper, if you can't follow that up by getting outside the building and finding ten people who will accept your higher price (your first milestone), then you have a problem! You don't need three years to figure this out. That is the power of this kind of estimation. You can quickly convert fuzzy revenue and profitability goals into more actionable innovation metrics that you can start validating immediately.

As you might have suspected, my quadrupled pricing model was met with some initial resistance. My target early adopters were typically software startup founders and they were used to spending $0–$100/month on third-party tools. A $200/month product was immediately perceived as outside the norm and expensive. In order to make my business model work, I needed a way to justify my higher pricing. Here's how I did this.

I noticed that my prospects were comparing my product to other third-party products in general (like their customer support software), which was an apples to oranges comparison. I realized that customers are not always good at determining the fair value of a product on their own and that you have to *explicitly anchor* your product against your customer's existing alternatives.*

While my customers were not spending hundreds of dollars a month on other analytics software, they were spending close to twenty hours/week on building out their own homegrown dashboards. Assuming a conservative $50/hour developer rate, $200/month represents just four developer hours/month. This is what I needed to effectively anchor my product. After grabbing the attention and interest of my prospects with a compelling demo, I shared my pricing model and followed with:

"I know that $200/month might be higher than most other services you are using, but given what you have seen (the demo), if you feel you can build something similar working just half a day a month, then you come out ahead and shouldn't buy our product."

This explicit anchoring technique was one of the key tactics that led to an 800 percent increase in conversion, from 10 percent when I first started presenting the higher pricing prospects to 80 percent a few weeks later.

What about testing customer lifetime values? Getting actual customer lifetime value numbers requires more time. But here also, you can begin to extrapolate

---

* For a great illustration of price anchoring at work, watch this video on how Steve Jobs unveiled the introductory price of the iPad: https://www.youtube.com/watch?v=QUuFbrjvTGw.

customer lifetime value using secondary approximations (like your monthly churn rate) without having to wait the full customer lifetime:

> Projected customer lifetime =
> 1 / (monthly churn rate)*

So, for example, a product that measures a monthly churn rate of 2 percent represents 1/0.02 = 50 months, or roughly four years of a customer lifetime. You don't have to wait four years to figure this out.

What About Ballparking More Complex Models?

I used a direct business model example, which is the simplest of the three types. Estimating the other two types of business models requires a few additional input assumptions but follows the same exact process:

1. Start with your minimum success criteria or desired throughput goal.
2. Convert this number to customer throughput.
3. Then refine and adjust the model.

MULTISIDED MODELS

Because users pay you with a derivative currency, the key difference here is calculating the value or exchange rate of this derivative currency.

---

* www.forentrepreneurs.com/saas-metrics-2-definitions/.

In the case of a product like Facebook, for instance, we calculate this derivative currency exchange rate as the average revenue per user (ARPU). You can get to this number by estimating the average cost per thousand impressions (CPM) advertisers will pay and the average monthly page views per user. Both these numbers are easily searchable online.

MARKETPLACE MODELS

With marketplace models, value is captured when a transaction is made. So the key difference is using the commission or transaction fee in your revenue stream to calculate the number of transactions per year you'll need to generate to sustain your minimum success criteria. You then estimate the number of buyers and sellers you will need in the system to sustain this transaction rate.

Exercise: Ballpark Your Business Model

Using your business model(s) from chapter 1, ballpark each one using the Fermi estimation method.

- Start with your minimum success criteria, which should be independent of your business model.
- Then, for each business model:
  - Estimate your customer lifetime value.
  - Convert your minimum success criteria into customer throughput.
  - Refine and adjust the model.
- Eliminate any models that don't work.

Key Takeaways

- If your business model doesn't work on paper, you'll be hard-pressed to make it work in the real world.
- Understanding the inputs versus the outputs to the model is what's actionable.
- You can ballpark the viability of a business model using a simple back-of-the-envelope estimation. Here are the steps:
  - Estimate your customer lifetime value.
  - Convert your minimum success criteria into a customer throughput rate.
  - Refine and adjust the model.
- A time-boxed traction goal is much more tangible than a revenue goal.

CHAPTER 3

Build a Traction Model

WHILE A CUSTOMER THROUGHPUT GOAL, LIKE THE ONE WE CALCU-lated in the last chapter, is a lot more concrete than a fuzzy revenue number, your minimum success criteria time box is still several years out into the future. We need a way to break this goal into smaller milestones. In *Running Lean* I offered a three-stage plan for doing this:

Each stage is driven by a high-level goal and a strategy for achieving it.

Stage 1—Problem/Solution Fit

> While ideas are cheap, acting on them is quite expensive.

The high-level goal of this stage is testing whether your idea represents a significant enough problem worth solving.

Earlier we saw some of the pitfalls of applying a build-first and/or a funding-first strategy at this stage. *Running Lean* instead advocated a traction-first strategy. You demonstrate traction not by building out a solution, but through the use of a proxy for your solution—something I call an "offer."

An offer is made up of three things: your unique value proposition, a demo, and pricing.

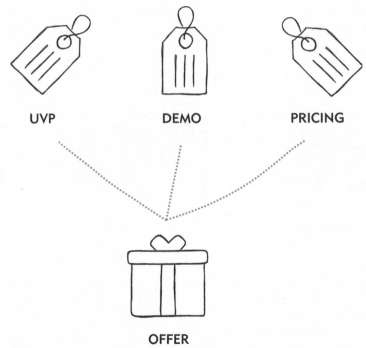

UVP   DEMO   PRICING

OFFER

1. A Unique Value Proposition

   This represents the finished story benefit or promise that you make to your customers to get their attention. If you were building a job-hunting site, for example, rather than rattling off your unique features, focus on what job seekers want: "Get a dream job in sixty days."

2. A Demo

   Your demo isn't intended to be just a collection of pretty screenshots or a working prototype, but rather a carefully scripted narrative that helps your prospects visualize your unique value proposition. It should walk them from their current reality (riddled with existing problems) to your envisioned future reality for them (one where these problems are solved with your solution).

3. A Pricing Model

   And finally, your offer should include an appropriate call to action. Depending on your business model type and the readiness of your solution, this may be an actual money exchange or some sort of derivative currency exchange.

Solution interviews, teaser landing pages, smoke tests, and crowd-funding pages are all examples of offer types you can use at this stage. You use your offer both to test for customer pull (a prerequisite for traction) and to refine your initial product specification (or minimum viable product), which prepares you for entering stage 2.

Note: Unlike other literature on minimum viable product (MVP), I draw a clear distinction between an offer and an MVP.

> It is not enough to measure what your prospects say—you have to measure what they do.

An MVP is the smallest solution that creates and captures monetizable value from users.

Stage 2—Product/Market Fit

The high-level goal of this stage is demonstrating your business model working at small scale. You need to demonstrate that you can both create value for your customers (through your solution) and capture some of this value back (through your revenue streams). The key insight here is that:

| You don't need lots of users, just a few good customers.

The strategy for doing this outlined in *Running Lean* employs fast and continuous feedback loops with customers for the purpose of iterating your MVP into a product that works.

Stage 3—Scale

> Perfect is the enemy of good.
>
> —VOLTAIRE

There is a marked shift in strategy at this stage from product to growth. This stage is less about driving your solution to perfection and more about finding the right engines of growth to realize the full potential of your business model.

While this high-level road map from *Running Lean* provided some guidance for navigating the highly uncertain terrain of innovation, it also raised additional questions such as:

What is the measurable goal of each stage?
How do you measure progress toward this goal?
When do you transition from one stage to the next?

Because each stage is characterized by a different strategy and goal, it is important to constantly locate yourself on your journey from ideation to scale. That is the job of your traction model.

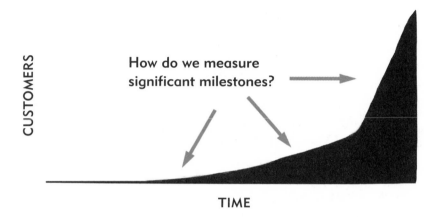

While your Lean Canvas describes your business model story, your traction model describes the desired output of your business model.

In order to build a traction model, we are going to first visit another key property of systems: repeatability.

> The traction model is to the financial model what the Lean Canvas is to the business plan.

Repeatability Enables Staged Rollouts

Once a system is in place, its throughput is predictable. A traditional factory, for instance, will output a set number of units per day within some tolerance for variability. This is the principle of repeatability.

The customer factory draws on this same principle. Now, you might say to yourself, a factory's output is predictable because it's powered by machines, and machines are largely consistent and predictable. Humans, on the other hand, are irrational and unpredictable. So how can we possibly expect predictability?

Dan Ariely is a professor of psychology and behavioral economics at Duke University. He is also the author of two best-selling books: *Predictably Irrational* and *The Upside of Irrationality*. As part of his research, he runs hundreds of experiments on how people make decisions—especially financial or purchase decisions.

Classical economics suggests that people make purchase decisions rationally after weighing all the potential upsides and downsides to the decision. Ariely's findings suggest otherwise. Chapter 5, "The Power of a Free Cookie," in his book covers the irrationality of free. When people are given multiple choices, including a free choice, the free option was the one most commonly exercised, even though it had an obvious downside. Getting something for free gave people such an emotional charge that they perceived what was being offered as a lot more valuable than it actually was.

> "... these irrational behaviors are neither random nor senseless—they are systematic and predictable."
>
> —DAN ARIELY, *PREDICTABLY IRRATIONAL*

In experiment after experiment, Ariely found that people will pick the same, poorer choice, which is indeed irrational. But here's the kicker: they were predictably so.

So even though humans may act irrationally, their behavior can be described by a model. You don't need lots of numbers to do this. In qualitative experiments, like usability tests, it has been shown that just five tests uncover 80 percent of all the issues. Similarly, after just ten customer interviews, you can often predict how the rest of your prospects will react to your offer.

Even once your product is launched, it's uncanny how the customer life cycle repeats itself day in and day out. Like clockwork, you start to observe predictable customer behavior in the number of people who visit your landing page, engage with your product, upgrade to become paying customers, or leave and never come back.

The Groundhog Day Effect

On the one hand, this kind of repeatability can be depressing. Because once steady traffic sets in, despite your best efforts, your charts flatline. No one wants to walk into a board meeting with a flatline graph.

On the other hand, repeatability in your business model can be highly empowering because it establishes the current benchmark of your customer factory. A stable benchmark gives you permission to aggressively experiment with bold new ideas with the goal of creating a spike in the flatline. If you do manage to create a spike, your next course of action is to run more of whatever you just did to make the spike stick at this higher level.

I call this the Groundhog Day effect—from the movie *Groundhog Day*, in which the protagonist played by Bill Murray is stuck in a loop where his life repeats itself every single day until he has a breakthrough insight that breaks the loop.

We entrepreneurs are similarly stuck in a daily loop of predictable customer behavior. Our job is to uncover the right breakthrough insights to move the curve up and to the right.

Growth as a Series of Steps

We often draw the hockey-stick curve as a smooth curve, but if you zoom in you'll find that it isn't so smooth after all. It is made up of a series of steps. Think of these steps as firing rockets that get you from one stable orbit to the next. Each of these firing rockets, or growth hacks, eventually burns out and needs to be constantly replaced with new ones. Each firing rocket represents a substrategy that got the business model from some initial customer throughput rate (point A) to a new customer throughput rate (point B).

Repeatability Before Growth

Not only is repeatability a property of systems, it is also a necessary precondition for growth. As part of my consulting practice, I advise entrepreneurs in accelerators who are usually working frantically on many things at once. I often find that they have a few paying customers, which is a great start.

My next question to them is: "Do you know how you're going to get your next ten paying customers?" Often they don't have a good answer.

You see, the first few customers came in from friends, others from adviser referrals, and the rest were seemingly random. The problem with random is that random is not repeatable.

My advice to them is to stop trying to go faster in every possible direction and instead slow down and try to figure out the repeatable pattern across their customers. The goal should be to identify a handful of actionable demographic and psychographic cues that triggered their purchase decision.

The reaction I often get is that we need to accelerate traction and go fast on everything. But accelerating on a plan that isn't yet repeatable just gets you lost faster.

Mark Suster, a VC who writes the popular blog *Bothsides of the Table*, published a great blog post titled "Invest in Lines, Not Dots," which captures this point perfectly.

> At the earliest stages, entrepreneurs need deceleration, not acceleration.

The thesis of the post is that a single data point in a product's trajectory, no matter how good it may be, is not investable. It's not enough to communicate progress because it isn't a rate.

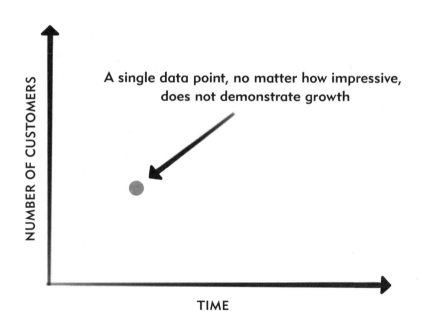

A single data point, no matter how impressive, does not demonstrate growth

You may have managed to achieve a one-time spike, for instance, by getting TechCrunched or doing a product launch at SXSW. A lot of companies used to scramble to secure investment after such a spike, but the more savvy investors know to wait and see if the spike sticks.

On the other hand, if you can demonstrate repeatability coupled with impressive customer throughput metrics even at microscale, you can extrapolate the business model story to paint a big picture.

This was the reason Facebook was able to command much higher valuations than its closest rivals, even though it had a lot fewer users and little revenue.

Facebook Won on Strategy

When Mark Zuckerberg started Facebook in 2004, he wasn't the only person building a social networking platform. There were dozens of other social networking platforms before his—many with millions of dollars in funding and millions of users. Yet he still managed to break into the market and build the largest social networking platform on the planet.

How did Facebook manage to win against bigger and better-funded competitors who had a huge head start? The answer: Facebook won on strategy—not on an original founding vision or an inherent unfair advantage.

While Facebook had a ballpark destination (set by its closest rivals), the most impressive aspect of its story was how it rolled out the product in stages.

While all his competitors had opened up their platforms to the public from day one, with the goal of growing as fast as possible, Mark did the opposite. He initially launched Facebook on just a single college campus—Harvard University. By initially limiting its launch to just a single college campus, Facebook was able to focus on first getting its product right without the distraction of having to also scale to millions of users at the same time (as its competitors did).

Staged rollouts prioritize testing customer risk over technical risk.

Within the first thirty days of launch, Facebook managed to demonstrate impressive user engagement metrics. Over 75 percent of Harvard students were on Facebook and more than half of them were logging in multiple times a day.*

Facebook then methodically rolled out its platform from one Ivy League university to the next, and eventually to other colleges. Not only did a staged rollout allow Facebook to play up exclusivity and desire, which was part of its overall strategy, but it had the more important effect of demonstrating repeatability in its business model. This was key to securing the investment capital it needed to grow. Facebook managed to raise just under $13 million within its first year of launching, with a postmoney valuation of more than $100M. Its two closest rivals, Myspace and Friendster, had both raised funding also at the end of their first year based on $46M and $53M, respectively.

While most of us on the outside were left scratching our heads, investors could already see the bigger picture of what Facebook had really built: a repeatable and predictable system for turning new, unaware students into happy, passionate users. It had built a **customer factory**.

Since Facebook's business model was multisided, these users represented a monetizable derivative asset whose value could be easily demonstrated. Facebook did this by using Google ads on its pages.

The inner workings of its customer factory allowed Facebook to go into any college campus and repeatedly demonstrate similarly impressive user engagement metrics to the ones on the Harvard campus. It didn't take much to extrapolate this superpower working on any college campus. Hence Facebook's high valuation.

After conquering most of the college campuses, Facebook set its sights beyond college students. It again employed a similar methodical staged rollout—this time launching from company to company before opening up to the public.

> You don't need lots of users to validate a business model.

—————
* Eighty-five percent of college students use Facebook (TechCrunch)—http://techcrunch.com/2005/09/07/85-of-college-students-use-facebook/.

By then it was unstoppable. It commanded another huge spike in valuation and secured enough capital to fuel its meteoric rise to the top of the social networking platforms.

Facebook achieved its goal of building the largest social network not by pursuing a land-grab strategy like its competitors but rather by following a carefully orchestrated staged rollout strategy. Even though it wasn't first and didn't start with an inherent unfair advantage, its staged strategy ultimately led Facebook to victory.

Building Out the Customer Factory in Stages

I used Facebook to illustrate the power of staged rollouts because everyone knows its story. And yes, Facebook is an outlier. Most startups don't grow as fast as Facebook did. That said, the principles behind staged rollouts don't work only at such a massive scale or only with viral products.

If you were charged with building out a real factory to manufacture a new widget, you wouldn't blindly crank up production to its highest level. You would probably first conduct some market demand analysis to determine an initial starting batch size. Then you would step up your factory production in stages—first running a few small batches to ensure that you could reliably manufacture your product before scaling up operations to meet market demand.

Building out any customer factory is no different. The first stage (Problem/Solution Fit) is where you test for sufficient customer pull to get the factory started. The other two stages (Product/Market Fit and Scale) are simply stepped-up versions of the first stage.

It's important to highlight that the goal of each stage isn't simply to create some set number of customers one time—for example, your first ten customers. Rather, the goal of each stage is to build a system that outputs a repeatable customer throughput rate, for example ten new customers a week. This, of course, begs the question: "What are the right customer throughput rates at each stage?"

Modeling Traction

We already have the required active number of customers needed for the scale stage. This was a number you calculated in the last chapter from your minimum success criteria.

In order to ballpark the other two stages, we are going to work backward from scale and create a time-boxed traction model for them.

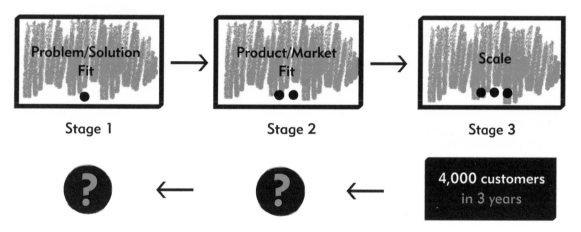

Work backward, starting here

STARTUPS DON'T GROW LINEARLY

The shortest distance between two points is a straight line, but startups don't grow linearly. To hit 4,000 customers in three years, you'll need to add 111 new customers every month starting from month one. This isn't realistic.

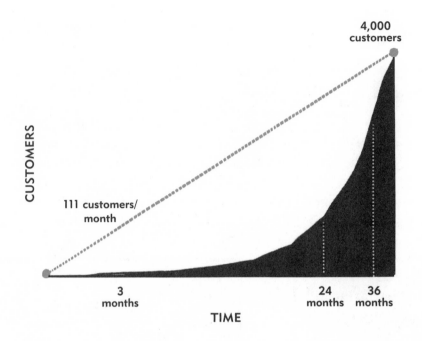

The hockey-stick curve tells a more realistic story. The flat portion of the hockey-stick curve provides a slower ramp at the beginning. You need this time to get your business model in order. The rate of growth (or the slope of the curve) picks up quickly from there. That's when the exponential part of the hockey-stick curve quickly outpaces a linear model. This slope is your measure of traction, or customer throughput.

STARTUPS DON'T GROW FOREVER

Even the hockey-stick curve is only part of the story. Business models don't grow forever. Either markets reach saturation or the business model gets disrupted. Even Facebook's user growth will reach saturation because there is an upper limit to the number of people on the planet (unless we start friending artificial intelligence [AI] bots).

A more accurate description of the business model trajectory is an S-curve, or the sigmoid function. The function was named in 1845 by Pierre François Verhulst, who studied it in relation to population growth.

We can map the three stages of a business model to this S-curve:

1. The Problem/Solution Fit stage is the flat portion of the curve when you validate customer demand for your value proposition.

2. The Product/Market Fit stage is the inflection point which marks the rapid or exponential growth stage of the business model.

3. Because it is hard to predict the saturation point of a market, I don't define the Scale stage as the top of the S-curve but rather the point when your minimum success criteria are met. You'll remember from chapter 2 that I recommend meeting your minimum success criteria goal using your early adopters, which leaves you room for further business model growth.

WHAT IS A GOOD GROWTH RATE?

Paul Graham, cofounder of the Y Combinator startup accelerator, defines a good growth rate as 5 to 7 percent a week. Here's a table from a blog post he published titled "STARTUP = GROWTH":

WEEKLY	YEARLY
1%	1.7x
2%	2.8x
5%	12.6x
7%	33.7x
10%	142.0x

It goes without saying that only a few outlier businesses can sustain these growth rates for a long period of time. A startup making $1,000/month and growing 5%/week will be making $25M/month in four years! Facebook's weekly revenue growth rate was 21.5% for the first six months and close to 5%/week for the next two years before the law of large numbers caught up to it and lowered its growth rate to ~1%/week.*

That said, while most businesses don't sustain these growth rates for long, I find that most successful businesses do start out this way. Y Combinator typically aims for hypergrowth startups that are somewhere between stage 2 and stage 3 and already generating some revenue from customers. Accounting for the earlier ramp-

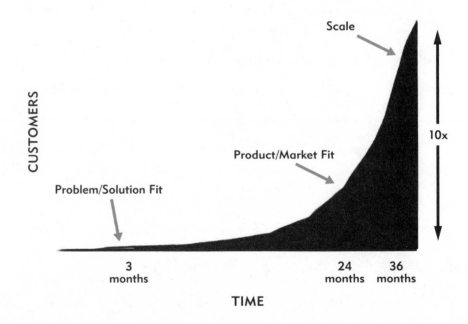

* www.quora.com/What-was-the-growth-rate-of-Facebook-year-by-year.

up period of stage 1, I simplified this 5- to 7-percent-a-week growth rate to a 10x rule that describes the trajectory of a startup from idea to minimum success criteria point.

> The 10x rule: The distance between the Scale stage and the Product/Market Fit stage is roughly an order of magnitude.

Venture capitalists Marc Andreessen[*] and David Skok[†] both use a similar 10x rule in the growth models for their portfolio companies. Like a Fermi estimate, the 10x rule isn't intended for significant precision but as a rough (yet good enough) ballpark. It works reasonably well for most products, but you should always check your own numbers to see if it aligns with your time line and high-level goals. Otherwise, adjust as needed.

WHAT IS A GOOD TIME BOX FOR THESE STAGES?

We have already established three years as the upper bound for your minimum success criteria goal, or the Scale stage. Let me cover the upper bound for the Problem/Solution Fit stage next.

Based on working with hundreds of entrepreneurs across a diverse range of products, I have found that the average time to go from idea to Problem/Solution Fit is eight weeks. Remember that at this stage, you don't build a product, but an offer, which allows for rapid validation. That said, the single biggest contributors to how long Problem/Solution Fit will take you are your willingness to get outside the building and your access to potential customers. For this reason, I place three months as the upper bound for achieving Problem/Solution Fit.

---

[*] Cofounder of Netscape and general partner of Silicon Valley venture capital firm Andreessen Horowitz.
[†] Five-time serial entrepreneur and partner at Matrix Partners in Boston.

Because the Product/Market Fit stage is one tenth of your Scale stage, following the 10x a year growth rule implies that you should reach this stage by year two.

USERcycle Case Study

Let's apply this model to the SaaS product we modeled earlier. For a $10M/year revenue run rate at the Scale stage, we had calculated the active customers count at roughly 4,000-plus customers. Applying the 10x rule, we can ballpark the other two stages as:

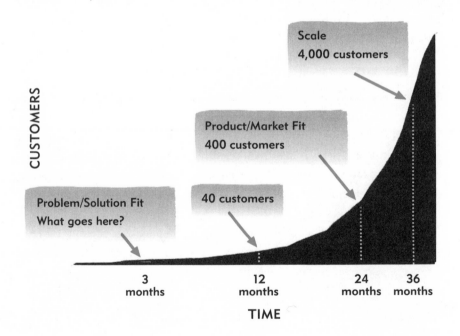

In this example, 4,000-plus customers/year at scale represented $10M revenue/year, so Product/Market Fit would be one tenth of that number. Achieving a $1M/year revenue run rate seemed like a reasonable transition point to shift from product to growth for this product, so I stuck with the numbers.

Where some further breakdown is usually needed is at the Problem/Solution Fit stage. At this stage, you are usually not yet creating customers, but leads or users, who are in the process of being converted to customers (through trials). So we need a way to turn the desired customer production rate to a leads or trials production rate.

If you don't have any better numbers to go on, use a power-of-ten estimation. I simply assumed that 10 percent of leads would convert to trials and 10 percent of trials would convert to customers.

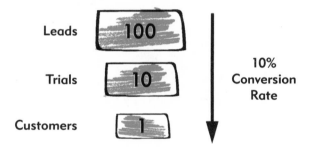

So in order to achieve a customer throughput rate of 40 customers/year by year one, I would need to generate $(40/12 \times 100)$ = 333 leads/month or $(40/12 \times 10)$ = 33 trials/month. I rounded the last number down to 30 trials/month, which became my Problem/Solution Fit success criteria.

You can probably appreciate now why you don't need three-digit precision in your calculations. Our goal is to take a big fuzzy number out in the future and turn it into something actionable and concrete in the present. Once you reduce your Scale number by a couple orders of magnitude, it becomes pretty actionable.

Facebook's Traction Model

Because Facebook wasn't first, it could rely on matching (and beating) the growth baseline set by its closest rivals. Here is what its initial traction model might have looked like given its original high-level concept of building a "Friendster for colleges":

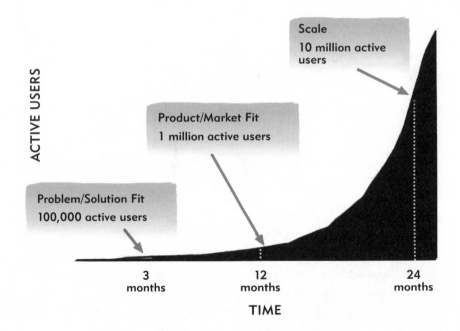

We all know that Facebook didn't stop there. It went on to do this:

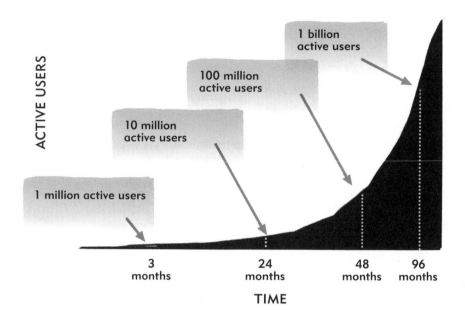

Why This 10x Strategy Works

Here's why this simple 10x model works:

YOU HAVE A SINGLE GOAL FROM IDEATION TO SCALE

Having a single-minded goal of increasing customer throughput brings clarity in your mission to build a successful product.

IT MAKES THE EARLY IDEATION STAGE MEASURABLE

The Problem/Solution Fit stage is the most qualitative of the three stages because it relies on data from smaller numbers of prospects usually gathered through interviews. For this reason, it's also considered the most uncertain. But using a systems approach, it doesn't have to be.

I run into lots of entrepreneurs who pat themselves on the back for conducting dozens of customer interviews, which I'll admit is commendable. But when I ask them "How many customers did you sign up?," the answer is usually disappointing, followed by "but I'm learning a lot." Then they point to their stacks of scribbled interview notes.

> While learning is a key activity, it's the results that matter.

Unless you can turn your learning into measurable results (measured as an increase in customer throughput), you are not making progress but simply engaged in a trivial pursuit. Rather than measuring the number of interviews or quality of interviews, focus instead on the macro goal of creating a customer (or as close to one as possible).

The way you do this during the Problem/Solution Fit stage is through your offer. Your prospects either accept or reject your offer. It's a binary decision.

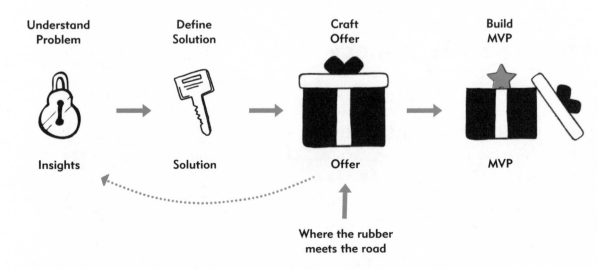

Understand Problem	Define Solution	Craft Offer	Build MVP
Insights	Solution	Offer	MVP

Where the rubber meets the road

THE 10X MODEL IS DECEPTIVELY SIMPLE

I often pose the same starting challenge to everyone irrespective of their business model type: "Can you find ten people who will use your product?"

The rationale for this challenge is that one of them will turn into a happy customer, which is the first singularity moment in a product's life cycle.

THE SINGULARITY MOMENT OF A PRODUCT

The singularity moment of a product is not when you write your first line of code or raise your first round of funding, but when you create your first customer. You go from nothing to creating value. Every business, whether it's Amazon, Google, or Facebook, started this way—with one before the millions (or billions). While one might seem too simple to strive for, it's not. In order to get one good customer, you need to get ten times as many people actively using your product. In order to get ten active users, you need to get ten times as many people interested in your product. So to get one good customer, you need to start with at least one hundred people. Not so easy after all . . .

When you are pursuing something new and innovative, people don't see what you see, which is the first battle. If you talk to ten people and none of them are interested in your idea, that is a statistically significant outcome that you need to address before tackling the thousands or millions of customers in your business model projections.

YOU ARE DONE ONLY WHEN YOU CAN DEMONSTRATE REPEATABILITY

I often see entrepreneurs come back with ten commitments from friends, which is a good start, but not yet a repeatable production rate. The exercise isn't about just talking to ten people once but building a system that you can repeatedly get tens of people interested in your product.

THE MODEL INCORPORATES PROGRESSIVE LEVELING UP

If you get this far, the next challenge is leveling up to getting hundreds of people interested, then thousands, and so on, until you reach your required Scale customer throughput rate.

While you might have employed customer interviews, for example, to secure tens of interested prospects, in order to get hundreds, you have to rewire your customer factory and level up your channels. In this case, you might hire additional salespeople or scale up by moving from a direct-sales model to a self-serve model through a marketing website.

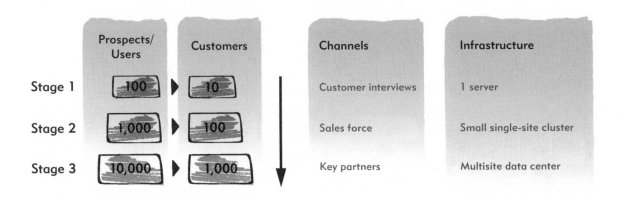

	Prospects/Users	Customers	Channels	Infrastructure
Stage 1	100 ▶	10	Customer interviews	1 server
Stage 2	1,000 ▶	100	Sales force	Small single-site cluster
Stage 3	10,000 ▶	1,000	Key partners	Multisite data center

You similarly have to level up on technical risk and other resources like your team.

10X EXPOSES THE RISKIEST PARTS OF YOUR BUSINESS MODEL

The 10x model automatically works to prioritize customer or market risk over technical risk.

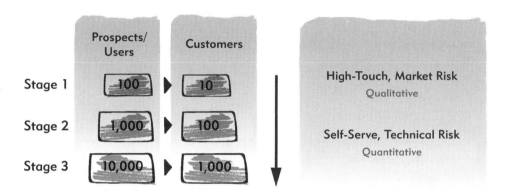

By purposely limiting your customer throughput batch size at the earlier stages, you can focus on finding the best early adopters for your product and on delivering the best possible high-touch experience to validate your value creation hypotheses. Your perspective on what you need to build (your solution) also changes. For instance:

- If you are building a software product, instead of waiting for your product to be usable to test your product, you could become the first user of your own solution, and offer its benefits as a consultant using a concierge MVP approach.

- If you are building a hardware product, instead of waiting for a fully automated manufacturing route, assemble your first 100 units by hand. This is what Pebble did.
- If you are building a low-tech product like starting a restaurant, instead of opening a brick-and-mortar restaurant, you could start with a food truck.

By embracing a smaller initial batch size of customers, you leave yourself no excuse not to succeed. This is what I call going for the easy button. The corollary is also true. If you can't deliver value to this small subset of your best possible customers, what makes you think you can deliver value to your hundreds or thousands of future mainstream customers?

HAVING A TRACTION ROAD MAP PROVIDES A GUIDING COMPASS

In my example above, I gave myself three months to achieve a production rate of 30 trials/month to achieve Problem/Solution Fit. If after month two, I have only 2 trials started, that indicates a red flag. If after month three, I am still off by a lot, that's my business model feedback loop telling me that I need to pivot or reset my approach.

THE 10X MODEL REQUIRES NONLINEAR THINKING

If, on the other hand, I achieve my goal of starting 30 trials/month, my next challenge isn't just maintaining this rate or even doubling it, but rather thinking of how to 10x this rate. Hypergrowth businesses don't grow linearly but in nonlinear steps. You have to think similarly.

Let's look at another example where a 10x rollout strategy is in play, not across a single product, but as a grand vision.

Tesla's 10x Strategy

Elon Musk had a big vision of moving us from a mine-and-burn hydrocarbon economy toward a more sustainable solar electric economy. A key part of this vision is building a mainstream, affordable, 100 percent electric car. But building an affordable all-electric car is a really hard problem. Instead of tackling it all at once, he employed a staged approach by first launching a high-performance electric sports car—the Tesla Roadster.

The biggest problem to solve for an all-electric car was range anxiety—that is, getting an electric car to closely match the stamina of a regular car on a full tank, which is usually around two to three hundred miles, depending on the type of car.

To prioritize solving this problem, Tesla didn't build a car from scratch. Instead it licensed the rights to use the body of another popular car: the Lotus Esprit. Tesla essentially took out the internals from the Lotus, fitted it with its own battery and motor, and sold it at a pretty high price tag.

The choice of body style wasn't random. It was carefully chosen to match both Tesla's positioning ("a performance electric car") and early adopters. By starting at the premium high end, Tesla was able to limit its scale of production and really focus only on getting the product right (i.e., to solve range anxiety by building better battery technology).

The next stage involved launching a more moderately priced (but still expensive) Model S. This car Tesla did build from the ground up. The company progressively scaled up its production capacity to do this, and this car too employed an interesting staged product rollout strategy.

Rather than changing the car configuration every year, like most car manufacturers, Tesla shipped every car packed with the same hardware and used over-the-air software updates to add new features. When the car first launched, for instance, it didn't have memory seats. That was added as a free software update. My favorite update story was when they made the car go four tenths of a second faster with just software. Imagine that.

This continuous deployment strategy allowed Tesla to bring its product more quickly to market and then use incremental updates to improve the product from there.

Beyond the Model S, Tesla now has its sights on introducing a mainstream vehicle priced at around $35,000, which may allow the company to realize its original vision for scale and impact. By that time, a lot of the product risk would have been mitigated and the infrastructure for scaling already built.

Exercise: Define Your Significant Success Milestones

For each of your business models,

1. Use the 10x rule to build a traction model.
2. Test the model so the numbers make sense for your business model type.

Key Takeaways

- Establishing repeatability in your business model is a prerequisite to pursuing growth.
- Growth is not a continuous function but a series of steps best described as firing rockets that get you from one stable orbit to the next.
- A staged rollout strategy works to automatically prioritize the right risks in your business model.
- You can break the product life cycle into three stages: Problem/Solution Fit, Product/Market Fit, and Scale.
- At a macro level, the only difference between the three stages is the customer throughput rate.
- The distance between each stage can be modeled using a 10x rule, which works both top down and bottom up.
- You can take on 10xing your business as a series of 2x steps.

PART 2
PRIORITIZING WASTE

Before you can prioritize waste, you have to
be able to see the factory floor.

Goal
Observe and Orient
Learn, Leverage, or Lift
Experiment
Analyze
Next Actions

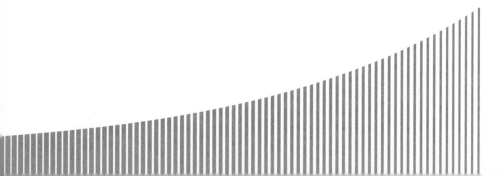

CHAPTER 4

The Customer Factory Blueprint

ATRACTION MODEL IS INVALUABLE WHEN YOU'RE CHARTING YOUR BUSIness model progress. But it's not as helpful for making day-to-day decisions. In other words, while measuring customer throughput can tell you whether you are on track, if you veer off course, it doesn't tell you how to course correct. For that we need to deconstruct traction further into additional metrics.

The common tendency with metrics is to collect and analyze as much data as possible. We live in a world where we can measure almost anything, but instead of getting clarity, we instead end up drowning in a sea of nonactionable data. If you have ever used Google Analytics, you know what I mean. Using a tiny snippet of JavaScript code, you can start collecting thousands of data points. Once you add a handful of other tools to the mix, these numbers quickly explode. Like too much information, too much data is paralyzing.

This problem is further exacerbated by the fact that the road to innovation is riddled with extreme uncertainty. At any given point in time, there are often myriad possible data points to consider and actions to take. Pareto's 80/20 principle still applies—80 percent of your results come from only 20 percent of your efforts. The key question, of course, is which 20 percent? The good news is that you don't need lots of numbers to figure this out.

Up until now, we have treated the customer factory as a black box and modeled

The customer factory blueprint deconstructs traction into its component steps.

its output only in our traction models. In this chapter we are going to take a trip inside this black box and lay out the full customer factory blueprint.

We are then going to apply another concept from systems thinking—the theory of constraints (TOC)—to prioritize the right 20 percent of actions. As with Taiichi Ohno's chalk circles, before you can draw them, you need to be able to see the factory floor.

The Happiest Place on Earth

Because earlier we established making happy customers the output of the factory, it is only fitting to use Walt Disney World as the first example, as it is supposedly the happiest place on the planet.

The customer factory blueprint shown opposite depicts the five-step process for making happy customers. These five steps are **acquisition, activation, retention, revenue, and referral**.

This blueprint describes the key macro steps that can be universally applied to any kind of business—one we will reference many more times throughout the rest of the book. Let's first walk through each of these steps using Disney World as our product.

1. Acquisition

   The factory represents your product or service. The initial battle is getting visitors inside your factory by building a path (or channel) to them. You may have the best product in the world, but if no one knows about it, your business model will be a nonstarter.

   This first step of turning unaware visitors into interested prospects is measured as **Acquisition**. This is the job of your offer. You'll remember that an offer

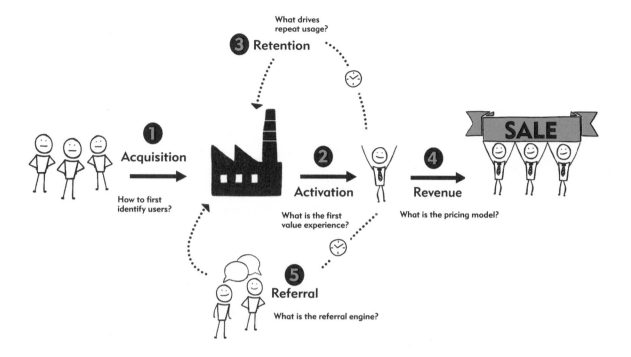

is made up of three things: a unique value proposition (or promise), a demo, and pricing (or a clear call to action).

In the case of a theme park, like Disney World, your unique value proposition might be promising an "unforgettable experience and a fun time," which you reinforce with your demo—delivered through images of happy people in your theme park. The call to action would be booking a trip.* You might use channels like advertising or travel agent partners to deliver this offer and drive traffic to your doorstep.

---

* Disney World does all three things on its landing page: https://disneyworld.disney.go.com/.

2. Activation

Once visitors are inside, the next battle is connecting your promise with the first user experience. This is measured as **Activation**. This step describes your first set of interactions with your users. Your goal should be closing the gap between your promise and the moment of first value creation (the aha moment) as quickly as possible.

If, for instance, people enter your theme park and find the first few rides broken, with people screaming and falling off them, that would represent a terrible first user experience. They would probably immediately ask for their money back and never return.

If, on the other hand, people are greeted with smiling faces and everyone else around them is happy (in line with your promise), your visitors would be tempted into staying inside your factory a bit longer.

3. Retention

The more time people spend inside your factory, the more value they potentially stand to create for themselves. This is a necessary precondition for being able to capture back value (or get paid) in the business model. The time people spend in your customer factory is measured as **Retention**.

Wait a minute, don't people pay before going to Disney World? While that is true, the basic sequence of value flow shown on the previous page still applies. Barring certain exceptions (like discounted or last-minute tickets), if a business fails to deliver on value, you are usually entitled to a refund.

> You have to first create value for your customers before you can capture some of it back.

In other words, if you fail to deliver on value, your customers will become unhappy and ask for their money back. So even though you might collect money up front, you don't necessarily get to keep it until you deliver sufficient value to your customers. This is true even if you have an online service. Online merchant account providers require that you maintain enough cash in your bank account so that you can honor any refunds and chargebacks from your dissatisfied customers.

It is equally important to highlight that not all retention is good retention. Simply keeping users inside your factory longer is not enough. If the amount of time people spend with your product does not correlate with value creation for them, they will start looking for other alternatives and consider leaving.

But if, on the other hand, value creation does track with time spent inside your factory, the longer they stay, the more value you stand to capture back from them. In a theme park, the more time people spend inside, the more money they potentially spend—on food, drinks, gifts, et cetera. Capturing back some of this value (or getting paid) is described by the next step.

4. Revenue

The **Revenue** step should be self-explanatory. It measures all the monetizable value captured back from your users.

In a direct business model, this is directly measurable in terms of money.

In a multisided model, value is first captured back from your users as a derivative asset. This value is then converted to money through your customers.

In a marketplace model, value is typically captured as a percentage of a transaction between buyers and sellers (as commissions and/or listing fees).

5. Referral

And finally, as you create happiness for your users, some of them will share their happy experience with others. This can be measured by the **Referral** step, which drives new visitors into your factory.

Most businesses have some kind of referral loop. Some businesses, like Facebook and Twitter, are inherently referral based (a side effect of using the product), others are more explicit when asking for referrals, and the rest simply rely on organic word of mouth.

Here too it's important to highlight the correlation between referral and value creation. Positive referrals track with value creation for your users. The opposite is also true.

> You have to create value for customers before you can truly earn a positive referral.

So these are the basic steps that describe the customer factory blueprint. This blueprint can be universally applied to any kind of business by simply mapping these macro steps to appropriate user actions. I'll illustrate this with a few additional examples.

Modeling a Flower Shop

Here's how you might map these five steps for a flower shop:

1. Acquisition

   Foot traffic outside your store represents potential visitors. When a passerby sees something interesting through your window display, she comes inside, which marks the **acquisition** action.

2. Activation

   Once she is inside, if the store has a bad smell or all the flowers are dying, that would represent a bad first experience that doesn't connect with the promise made outside the store. The person would probably turn around and leave.

   If, on the other hand, the inside of the store connects well with your window display, you deliver a compelling first experience and **activate** the user.

3. Retention

   Even activated visitors may not be ready to buy anything on their first visit, but you can still track time spent in the store and count their future visits as **retention**. People repeatedly coming back serve as a leading indicator for future monetization, which is the next step.

4. Revenue

Some of these visits will turn into actual purchases, which we measure as money spent or **revenue**.

5. Referral

Finally, if the customer likes your store enough, she might tell her friends. You might even facilitate this exchange by giving her a coupon to share with others. All these behaviors serve to drive more new visitors to your store through the **referral** trigger.

Modeling a Web Application

In the case of a Web application, all the people who hit your landing page are visitors to your site who can come from a variety of traffic sources.

1. Acquisition

Some of these people will leave right away; others will spend some time looking around and decide to sign up for your service. This marks the **acquisition** event.

2. Activation

Once they are signed up, if your application is too confusing or doesn't deliver on the promise made on the landing page, users will leave.

If, on the other hand, your app delivers on value and gives users a compelling reason to come back, you mark them as **activated**.

3. Retention

Retention measures time spent with your application on the first and future revisits. Every time the user comes back to your site, that triggers a

retention action. Ideally, you also want to ensure that users aren't just returning because your app is hard to use and that they are realizing value with each visit.

4. Revenue

Any direct monetization (like purchases or subscription upgrades) would be measured as **revenue** actions. If instead your users generate a derivative asset, you would appropriately track the derivative user currency, such as the number of page views or user-generated content created by a user, in lieu of actual payment.

5. Referral

Finally, you might employ a number of referral tactics, such as social media share buttons, referral codes, et cetera, to drive new visitors to your application. All these would be tracked using the **referral** trigger.

Modeling a One-Time-Use Product

What about one-time-use products like a book? All the steps still apply.

You drive visitors to your book landing page through your channels (**acquisition**), where they get **activated** after reading a sample chapter, for instance. After purchasing your book (**revenue**), repeated readings (**retention**) reinforce the promise of your book. This prevents them from returning the book, may drive positive word of mouth (**referrals**), and even purchases of your future books.

Certain types of businesses do predominantly have a one-time-usage model—making retention more short-lived. Take a divorce lawyer, for example. I think it's safe to say that it wouldn't be prudent for a divorce lawyer to build his business model around repeat business. It would be more prudent for him to leverage the referral trigger.

Macro Versus Micro Metrics

As you might have noticed already, all of the steps in the customer factory blueprint are really macro events that mark the most significant actions your customers take. These macro events are usually made up of one or more additional micro events. For instance, before someone shows up at Disney World (acquisition), they might have to click an ad, visit a landing page, and browse around before deciding to go.

The purpose of the blueprint is not to capture every substep—just the most significant customer life-cycle events. These significant customer life-cycle events are enough to visualize the customer factory that powers your business model. Using fewer numbers not only keeps you from drowning in numbers, but as you'll see in the next couple of chapters, it also helps drive focus on the right hot spots in your business model. Much as we rely on a few standard financial metrics to measure the performance of well-established companies, we can similarly use these few customer factory metrics to measure the performance of a startup.

The Pirate Metrics Funnel

You might have recognized the steps in the customer factory blueprint from Dave McClure's Pirate Metrics model. That model describes the customer life cycle as a marketing funnel. For those of you wondering why it is called Pirate Metrics, the first letters of each of the steps spell out "AARRR," which is something pirates like to say.

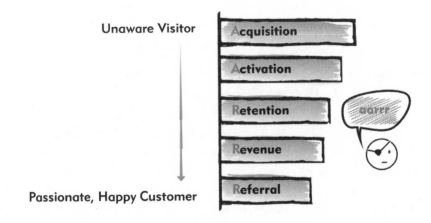

Unaware Visitor

Passionate, Happy Customer

Acquisition

Activation

Retention

Revenue

Referral

aarrr

I have been using the Pirate Metrics model for a number of years now, but decided to present it differently in this book for a variety of reasons.

1. The customer factory flow is nonlinear.

The funnel view assumes a linear flow for converting visitors into customers when in fact the process is nonlinear. One gripe that a lot of people have with the Pirate Metrics representation is where to place the referral step: before or after revenue?

Because referrals directly correlate with value creation or happiness, it's much more natural to visualize referrals in the customer factory as a feedback loop leading out of the value creation step.

2. The customer factory incorporates emotion.

Most funnel representations (and spreadsheets) show only numbers and percentages and lack emotion. Emotion is a powerful driver in the customer life cycle that shouldn't be ignored. The simple use of people icons and the emphasis on happiness (or not) in the customer factory blueprint is a subtle reinforcement that metrics are people first.

3. The customer factory simplifies complex concepts.

Finally, because the customer factory blueprint is more visual than a funnel, it makes it easier to describe complex concepts. Notice, for instance, that there are two hot-spot nodes in the diagram:

i. The value creation step: This is the one showing people with their hands up in the air. It is also the node with the greatest number of lines leading out from it.

ii. The customer factory: This is the node with the greatest number of lines leading into it.

We'll cover the significance of each next.

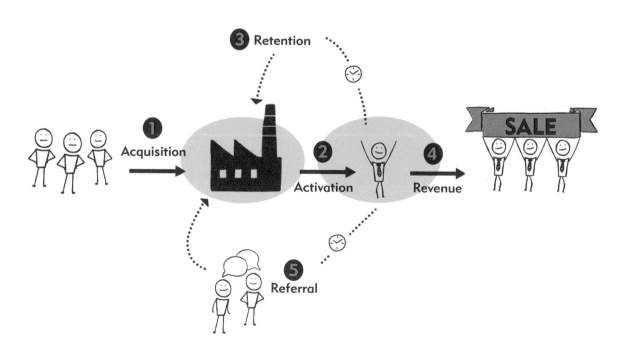

The Happy Customer Loop

Because the value creation step has the greatest number of arrows leading out of it, it represents a causal step in the blueprint.

Creating happiness (or delivering results) for your customers causes them to

- Spend more time with your product (retention),
- Create more monetizable value (revenue), and
- Spread goodwill about your product (referral).

The inverse is also true.

Creating unhappiness for your customers causes them to

- Leave your product (retention),
- Ask for a refund (revenue), and
- Leave negative reviews on your product (referral).

For this reason, this step is also the most reliable leading indicator for traction. We can take this even further and draw a happy customer loop as shown on the opposite page.

When you first launch a product, the happy customer loop is where most of your attention should be placed. Your first user experience and subsequent user visits serve as leading indicators for revenue (monetization) and referrals. Let's turn next to the node with the greatest number of inbound connections.

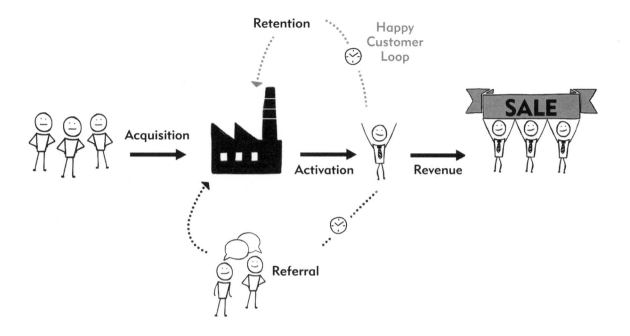

Engines of Growth

It shouldn't be surprising that the customer factory is the node with the most lines leading into it. These inbound connections drive more people into your factory and describe the engines of growth for increasing customer throughput.

1. PAID ENGINE OF GROWTH

This engine utilizes the acquisition trigger to drive more visitors into your factory. It is called a paid engine because you typically have to pay for this kind of growth. It might require hiring additional salespeople or buying advertising. Even if you rely solely on social media, that still falls under the paid engine of growth because it costs time (and money) to manage.

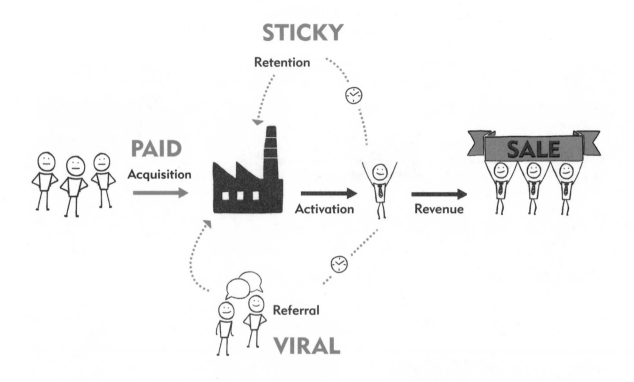

The paid engine is sustainable when the monetizable value captured from your customers (LTV) exceeds the cost of creating a customer (COCA).

For a healthy business, you should aim for a 3x ratio between LTV and COCA. This ratio is attributed to David Skok, a five-time serial entrepreneur and partner at Matrix Partners in Boston. He regularly shares his insights on his popular blog *forEntrepreneurs* and has validated this ratio across many SaaS businesses.*

---

* SaaS Metrics, David Skok: forentrepreneurs.com/saas-metrics/.

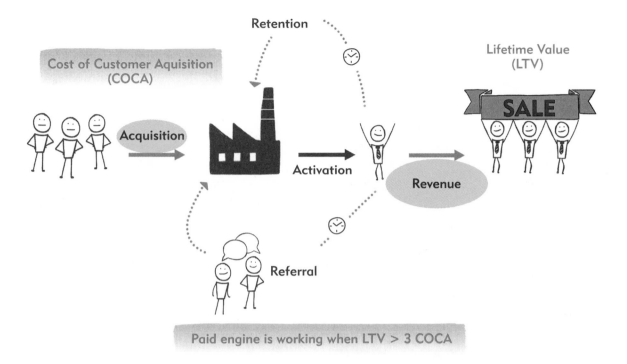

Cost of Customer Aquisition (COCA)

Retention

Lifetime Value (LTV)

Acquisition

Activation

Revenue

SALE

Referral

Paid engine is working when LTV > 3 COCA

2. STICKY ENGINE OF GROWTH

This engine utilizes the retention trigger to keep users inside your factory longer. The more time they spend with your product, the more value you're potentially able to deliver to them—which should then translate to more captured value.

Stickiness can be achieved organically or through enforced lock-ins. Organic stickiness is a side effect of delivering a compelling value proposition or repeatedly getting a job done. People stick around until the job they hired your product to do is completed. Enforced lock-ins are typically enacted through contracts. Examples are mobile plans and magazine subscriptions.

This engine is sustainable when the number of customers outputted by your factory (customer throughput rate) exceeds the number of customers lost due to churn.

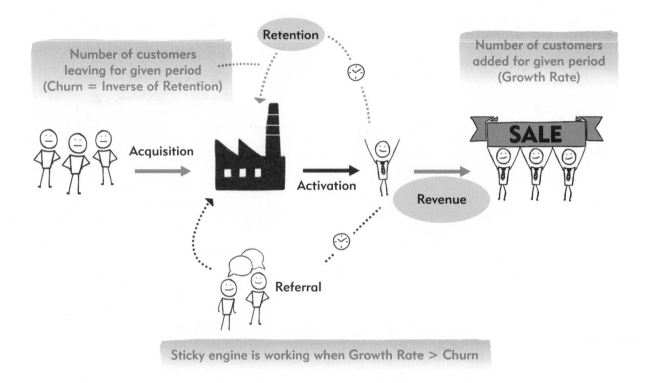

Number of customers leaving for given period (Churn = Inverse of Retention)

Retention

Number of customers added for given period (Growth Rate)

Acquisition

Activation

Revenue

SALE

Referral

Sticky engine is working when Growth Rate > Churn

3. REFERRAL ENGINE OF GROWTH

This engine utilizes the referral trigger. The goal here is to have your happy customers refer new visitors into your factory who then go on to become customers. This can take many forms, from basic word-of-mouth marketing to elaborate affiliate and incentive-driven campaigns.

The referral engine is working when the average customer referral rate is greater than zero.

People loosely use the term "viral," but viral has a very specific definition. In

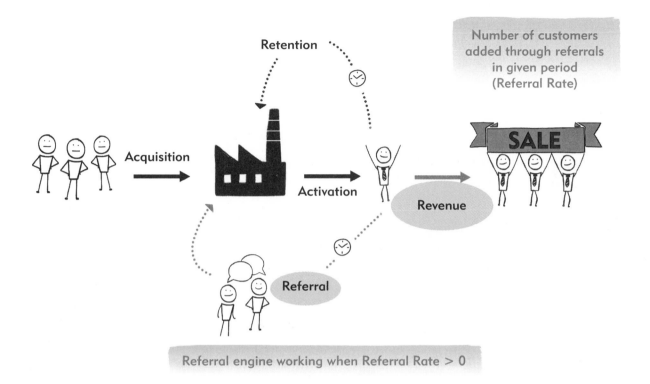

Retention

Acquisition

Activation

Revenue

Referral

SALE

Referral engine working when Referral Rate > 0

order for a product to be considered viral, it needs to have an average referral rate of over 100 percent. In other words, every customer should on average be referring at least one other customer to your factory. It's easy to see how the viral engine of growth is the fastest growth engine.

Also contrary to popular belief, going viral is not something you can predictably plan. Sure, you can encourage referral behavior by adding easy share options, but you can't force viral customer behavior.

As you have probably figured out, it is theoretically possible to apply more than one engine of growth to a business model. But at any given time, a single engine will probably stand to give you the highest return on investment. We'll cover how to pick one later in the book.

Customer Throughput Versus Throughput

In chapter 1, I made the subtle, yet important, distinction between customer throughput and throughput.

Customer throughput measures the rate at which you create customers, while throughput measures the rate at which you create monetizable value from your customers.

The goal of a business is increasing throughput, which is not always the same as increasing customer throughput. Simply adding more customers will also drive up more inventory and operating expenses. You might be able to potentially drive up throughput by increasing prices instead.

Before applying an engine of growth to drive up your customer throughput, you usually have to first optimize the throughput levers in your customer factory. These levers are:

1. The batch size of users you allow into your customer factory.
2. The conversion rates of each of the five macro steps,
3. The time between conversions (or cycle time), and
4. Your monetization (or pricing) model.

Optimizing these traction levers gets you to a business model that works, which you then scale by firing up one or more engines of growth.

Exercise: Sketch Your Customer Factory Blueprint

For each of your business models, map each of the five customer factory steps to a key user action you can track as I illustrated in the examples above. You can download a worksheet for this exercise at http://LeanStack.com/customer-factory.

1. Visitors

    Starting on the left, list the inputs to your customer factory as the acquisition channels listed on your Lean Canvas.

2. Acquisition

    For the acquisition step, identify the point when you identify visitors as "real" people. As an example, for a Web-based product, I typically prefer using the point when I first get a unique user identifier, like an e-mail address.

    I recommend collecting e-mail addresses versus just opaque identifiers (like user names) because an e-mail address lets you have a two-way conversation with your visitors. You can also extract additional information from just an e-mail address, such as the company name (if it's not a personal e-mail address), and even run it through third-party services, like FullContact, to get richer social profile information.

    You may not always be able to collect e-mail addresses up front. In those cases you could still identify users using user names and even cookies on your site. It's not as robust and useful as an e-mail address, but it still works.

3. Activation

Next, define your activation event. This is ideally the point when your users have their first aha moment with your product. Think: taking your first ride in a theme park.

In the Lean Canvas tool, we currently define this aha moment as when people complete at least 70 percent of the canvas. Twitter found that its aha moment is when people start following at least ten people. Write down the first aha moment for your product.

4. Revenue

Revenue shouldn't require much explanation. These are the points where you collect money from customers. Put down your pricing model from your Lean Canvas.

5. Retention

If you have a retention component to your service, identify how you might track this event. On a website or online app, this can be as simple as tracking the number of repeat users coming to your site.

Also list your projected customer lifetime. This is the number you came up with in your back-of-the-envelope customer throughput calculation exercise.

6. Referral

Write down any referral triggers you could employ. This could be as simple as word of mouth or social sharing for now. If you have referral built in as a side effect of using your product (as Facebook and Twitter do), list what actions drive sharing and how you might track them.

7. Throughput Goal

Finally, write down your desired customer throughput goal.

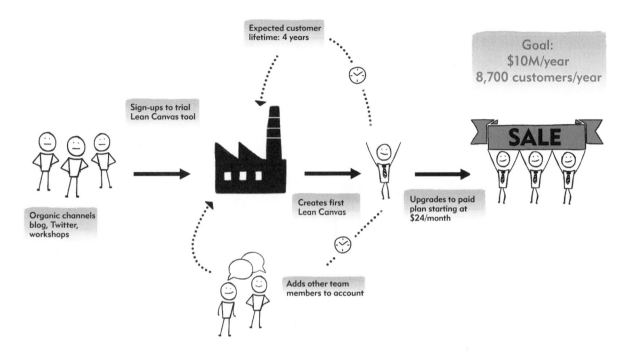

Expected customer lifetime: 4 years

Goal: $10M/year 8,700 customers/year

Sign-ups to trial Lean Canvas tool

SALE

Organic channels blog, Twitter, workshops

Creates first Lean Canvas

Upgrades to paid plan starting at $24/month

Adds other team members to account

Congratulations! You have successfully created the basic customer factory blueprint for your business.

Where Is the Constraint?

Okay, so now that we have deconstructed the customer factory, we are ready to start identifying constraints. Where would you say is the first constraint or weakest link in the system?

Sorry, that was another one of my trick questions. We can't really answer this question until we have more data. All we have done so far is design and wire up all

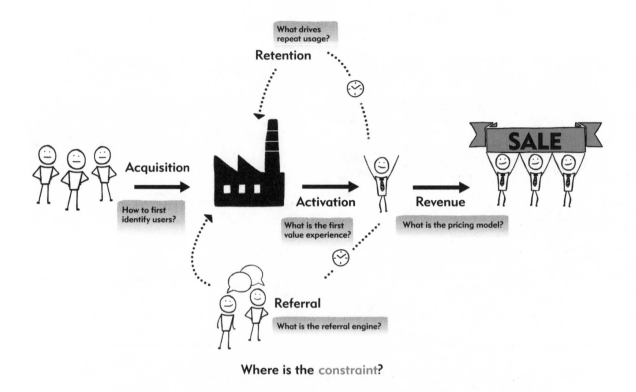

Where is the constraint?

the machines on our factory floor, but we haven't flicked the switch on. The factory starts running only once you start driving visitors (or raw materials) to your factory doorstep by way of your offer (landing page, sales call, webinar, etc.). Contrary to popular belief, flicking the switch on is a lot easier than most people think.

With all the ad networks, social networks, and your own personal referral network, there is an abundance of traffic. You can probably drive enough starting traffic to your landing page or find enough people to interview. The bigger challenge, of course, is getting these visitors to take the next step—to "convert" into interested prospects and enter your customer factory.

> You don't usually have a traffic problem, but a conversion problem.

Testing this conversion is essentially the goal of the Problem/Solution Fit process outlined in *Running Lean,* where you drive visitors into your customer factory using your offer (as a proxy in place of a fully built-out solution) and aim to convert sufficient visitors into customers (as defined by your 10x Problem/Solution Fit criteria).

The logic here is that if you can't drive sufficient visitors into your customer factory, none of the other steps in the customer factory blueprint matter. It doesn't matter how good your solution is, or what referral incentives you build. No one will ever get to them.

So if you answered "acquisition" to the question above, you were on the right track, because that's the first prerequisite step. While most entrepreneurs set out to overcome a bunch of internal constraints (like team, money, and product), starting constraints in any system are almost always external. The customer factory is no different.

First, does a market *really* exist for your product? When modeling a business, we usually assume market demand to be some nonzero percentage of our total addressable market captured as customer segments on the Lean Canvas. Otherwise it wouldn't make any sense to pursue the idea. But this still needs to be tested.

So while flicking the customer factory switch on is the obvious next action, things get trickier after that. There can be myriad reasons why your users don't convert after that: customer segmentation issues, pricing, channel issues, et cetera. Before you can identify the right next constraint, you have to benchmark your customer factory—which is the topic of the next chapter.

> When you get hit by an idea, rushing to first build out your solution or to find investors is premature optimization.

Key Takeaways

- Before you can prioritize waste, you need to be able to see the factory floor.
- You can visualize the customer factory using five steps: acquisition, activation, retention, revenue, and referral.

- Acquisition, or turning unaware visitors into prospects, is often the initial battle.
- The next challenge typically is activation and retention, or getting users around the happy customer loop.
- Focus then shifts to growth, which can be triggered by scaling up acquisition, retention, and referrals.

CHAPTER 5

Benchmark Your Customer Factory

WE NOW HAVE A SIMPLE BLUEPRINT FOR DECONSTRUCTING TRACTION into its component steps. In this chapter, we're going to cover how to use this model to benchmark the "true progress" of your business model.

Don't Feed Your Vanity

One of the reasons measuring "true progress" is hard is that we prefer reporting good news over bad news. We like charts that trend up and to the right, which isn't all that bad by itself—until we start devising charts that can go nowhere but up and to the right.

Cumulative counts, like the total number of people who have ever signed up for your service, regardless of whether they continue to use it, are the perfect example. While these numbers can flatline, they can never go down. That's the first telltale sign that you have a vanity metric on your hands.

Here's an example graph plotting sign-ups (acquisition) in two different ways. Both charts use the same underlying data set, but each tells a different story.

> It is not the metric itself, but how you measure it, that makes it a vanity or an actionable metric.

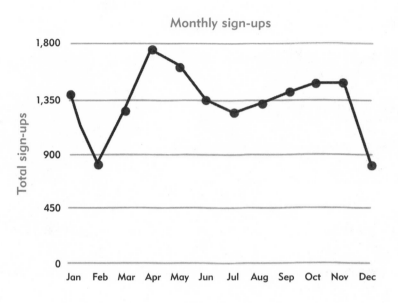

Monthly sign-ups

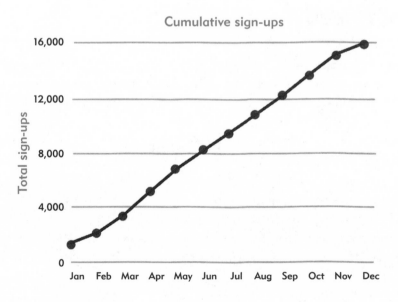

Cumulative sign-ups

To be fair, there is a place for vanity metrics. They can be used with great effect on marketing websites to build up social proof and ward off competition. But when you use these same metrics as internal measures of progress, they provide only an illusion of progress and prevent you from confronting brutal facts about your business.

Strive for Actionable Metrics

We also get into trouble when we gravitate toward measuring things the easy way—for example, measuring metrics in aggregate versus in batches (or cohorts). Measuring metrics in aggregate is where we simply count the number of occurrences of significant events within a particular reporting period (like the number of website hits) versus tracking them by user. The pro of this approach is that it's simple to do. The con is that it isn't always accurate.

While measuring customer behavior in aggregate is a quick measure of how your business is doing, the issue is that some user actions (like revenue) are long-life-cycle events. When you simply count events that occur within a one-month interval, you are mixing events from different users at different stages in their life cycle, which often leads to inaccurate metrics—especially when your product is also constantly changing.

Consider a scenario where there is a traffic spike in the number of sign-ups in a particular month. If you simply measure your revenue conversion rate as the ratio of the number of users who upgraded in a given month to the number of users who signed up in that month, your revenue conversion rate will appear to have dropped significantly in the current month and be abnormally high in the following month.

During this time, your product is also constantly changing with every feature release and marketing campaign. The danger is misplacing attribution of cause and effect and reaching the wrong conclusion.

For a metric to be actionable, you additionally need to be able to derive causality.

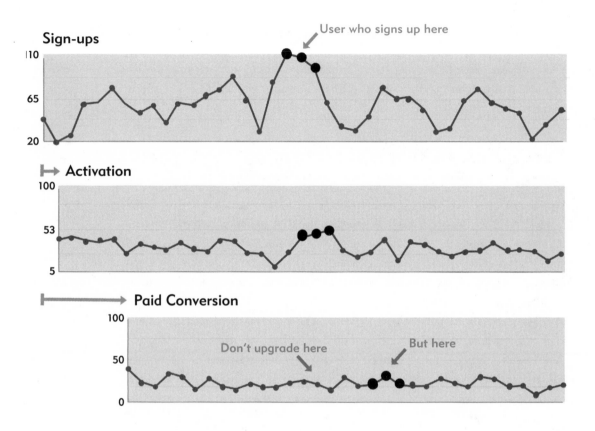

The gold standard for doing this is measuring your customer life cycle in batches (or cohorts).

What Is a Cohort?

Let's say you wanted to study the effect of college education on salaries. You have access to data collected over a one-year period that shows the starting salaries of people who have a college education. If you also have data on people without a college education, you could quickly create an average salary for both and determine whether people with a college education command a higher salary.

Average Salary

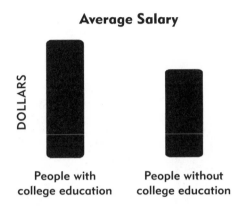

What if you then wanted to determine whether colleges are getting better? Even with additional years of aggregate salary data, this would be hard to determine accurately because the data set would contain everyone who ever got a college education. You would have no way of telling apart people who just graduated from those who got a degree five years ago. You end up with an averaging effect across the years.

Average salary of people with college education

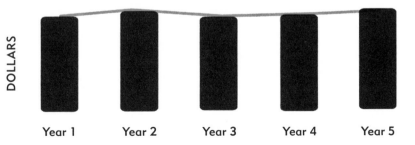

If, on the other hand, you had the additional field of their graduation year, you could then group the data into cohorts by graduation year and calculate a new starting salary average. By comparing this average across different graduation years, you would be able to determine whether the effect of a college education on starting salaries is improving.

Average starting salary of recent graduates

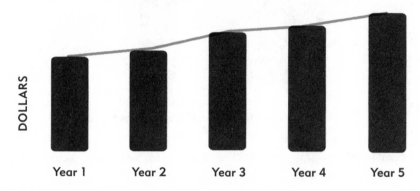

This subgrouping of all salary data into starting salaries of recent grads is an example of a cohort. It allows you to isolate the effect of a variable under study by isolating the population most recently affected by that variable (when they graduated from college, in this case).

Cohorts help you measure relative progress by pitting one batch of users against another.

Much as measuring the total population as an aggregate drives down the average salary toward the same point, similarly measuring the total population of your users will drive down your metrics toward an average that delays studying the true effects of your experimental efforts—like launching a new feature or marketing campaign.

Measure Throughput in Batches

The concept of batches is even easier to understand with the factory metaphor. Daily-run baselines build on the principle of repeatability and help factory managers quickly detect problems on the factory floor. When a particular batch yields abnormal results, they not only know something is wrong, but they can also quickly home in on the problem step.

You can take the same approach to benchmarking a customer factory. You start by grouping your users into daily, weekly, and monthly batches based on their join date (or sign-up date). Then measure their significant user actions as they progress through your customer factory.

The screenshot on the next page shows a normalized monthly view from one of my other products (Lean Canvas).

Each of these monthly slices tracks actions only by users who joined in those respective months. Some of these actions might have occurred in future months (like revenue) but they are still attributed to the user batch based on their join date.

Notice how several numbers have flatlined. I described this as the Groundhog Day effect earlier. This flatlining wasn't because we weren't working hard to improve these numbers. During this time, we were pushing out all kinds of features but nothing was working. Later in the book, I'll share the story of how we managed to uncover a breakthrough insight (using the principles in this book) that turned the trajectory of these numbers upward.

While measuring your metrics as cohorts is more work than simply measuring them as an aggregate, a cohorts-based approach affords the following benefits, which make it worth the extra effort:

1. It isolates product changes.

    If you think of your product as a moving river that is constantly changing, grouping users by their join date groups them into batches that experience

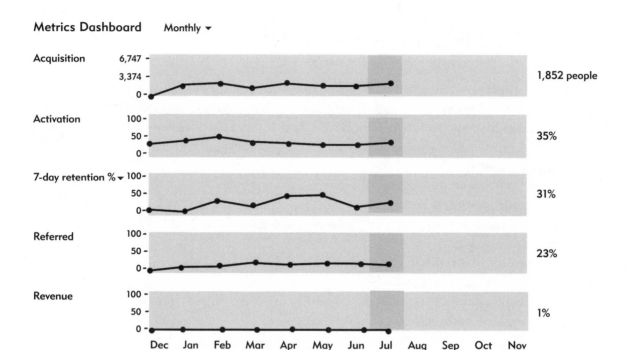

Metrics Dashboard   Monthly ▾

Acquisition	6,747 – / 3,374 – / 0 –	1,852 people
Activation	100 – / 50 – / 0 –	35%
7-day retention % ▾	100 – / 50 – / 0 –	31%
Referred	100 – / 50 – / 0 –	23%
Revenue	100 – / 50 – / 0 –	1%

Dec   Jan   Feb   Mar   Apr   May   Jun   Jul   Aug   Sep   Oct   Nov

your product similarly enough. Together they establish a baseline or benchmark to beat.

This concept of grouping users by a common attribute can be extended beyond join dates. You can create cohorts by gender, acquisition traffic source, release dates, a feature they use, et cetera.

2. It makes it easier to visualize progress.

Comparing the relative throughput of different batches over time provides you with an apples-to-apples comparison. Once you normalize your data and track users as cohorts, numbers moving up and toward the right are no longer vanity metrics—they are an accurate measure of progress.

3. It homes in on causality.

If you do see a spike across your batches, it allows you to home in on possible causes by inspecting what changed in the batch. Your next job is to further isolate the effect of that action, possibly by repeating that action and looking for similar results. This is the basis of split testing (also referred to as A/B testing).

HubSpot Case Study

Like many companies, HubSpot pays its salespeople by commission. It noticed that most sales close during the last week of the month. This is typical at most companies, as salespeople tend to push harder at the end of the month to meet their quotas. Do customers closed at the start of the month behave differently from customers closed at the end of the month?

To study this, HubSpot started measuring its customer life cycle in weekly batches grouped by their close date. By viewing the data this way, the company could quickly see that customers who closed at the end of the month were much more likely to also churn (or cancel) the following month. Further investigation revealed that these customers often resulted from aggressive sales tactics. While HubSpot's salespeople were optimizing for short-term goals (meeting their sales quotas), they were inadvertently hurting the macro goal (of increasing throughput).

HubSpot's solution was to make salespeople accountable for short-term churn. It implemented a Customer Happiness Index (CHI) that measured which parts of the product a customer was using and awarded weighted scores to each. For instance, usage that led to better business outcomes for customers had more weight.

> Engaged or happy customers churn less.

These CHI scores served as a leading indicator helping HubSpot's salesforce to identify "at-risk" customers and proactively attempt to prevent them from churning. By tying sales commissions to CHI scores (versus the close of a sale), the company was able to realign focus on the right macro goal of making happy customers.

The Downside of Cohorts

Apart from being harder to measure, a more practical downside of cohorts is that—because they measure the actual customer journey—you need to wait for all the data to be in for the results to be accurate.

For a thirty-day trial product, for instance, while you might get a few upgrades before the thirty-day mark, most people wait until the last day. To measure the effective conversion rate for a given month, you have to give everyone thirty-plus days, which requires waiting up to sixty-plus days for users who joined at the beginning of a month for the whole cohort to complete.

You can use aggregate metrics to generate a rough projection that you subsequently verify with cohorts.

One way to overcome this issue is to measure your batches using smaller windows, like weekly and even daily batches. Another way is to rely on a hybrid approach: using a combination of aggregate and cohort metrics.

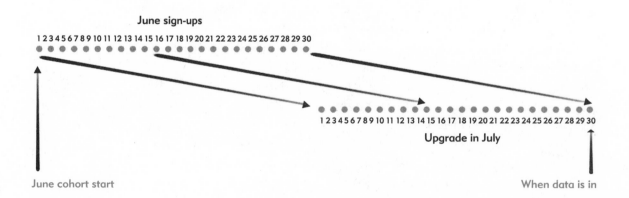

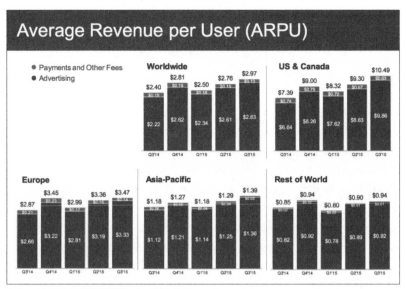

Source: Facebook Q3 2015 Earnings Results

Any data is generally better than no data. Aggregate metrics calculated over a long enough period of time are still helpful in establishing baselines. Facebook, for instance, calculates its quarterly average revenue per user (ARPU) by dividing its total advertising revenue that quarter by the number of active users in that quarter. This gives Facebook a quick and simple measure of progress.

That said, not all users are equally active, and not all ads convert equally either. In order to understand these effects, Facebook needs to dig deeper, and segmenting its users into batches is the gold standard for doing this.

Exercise: Baseline Your Throughput

You are now ready to benchmark your business model throughput.

1. Pick a reporting window.

    You should ideally measure your customers in daily, weekly, monthly, and eventually quarterly and yearly batches. I recommend starting with weekly batches.

2. Gather the numbers.

    While there are lots of great third-party tools for measuring the various steps in the customer factory blueprint, I haven't yet found a single tool that works across the full customer factory blueprint. As a result, we end up using a number of different tools to piece together our metrics dashboard. If you're just starting out and in the Problem/Solution Fit stage, I don't even recommend investing in an elaborate third-party tool. A combination of Google Analytics and manual tracking of user actions (like e-mail response rates and interview calls to action) is usually enough.

3. Assemble your companywide dashboard.

    Even though you might use different tools to measure different steps in your customer factory, it is still a good idea to summarize the big picture on a single page. You can download a simple fifty-two-week customer factory template here: http://leanstack.com/52-week-customer-factory-template.

"A business should be run like an aquarium, where everybody can see what's going on."

—JACK STACK, *THE GREAT GAME OF BUSINESS*

Having a single companywide dashboard helps to align your team around the most pressing hot spots or constraints in your business model. Identifying these constraints is the topic of the next chapter.

Key Takeaways

- Avoid vanity metrics as internal measures of progress.
- Create a companywide dashboard that answers the question: Are we making progress?
- Measure your customer factory in daily, weekly, and monthly batches.
- Create a dashboard that you share with everyone in the company.

CHAPTER 6

Finding Constraints

NOW THAT WE HAVE A WAY OF VISUALIZING THE FACtory floor, we are finally ready to start drawing chalk circles to give us a vantage point from which to learn about hidden sources of waste.

Let's dig further into the theory of constraints as it applies to a factory floor. Below are five steps taken inside the factory, each finished at varying speeds.

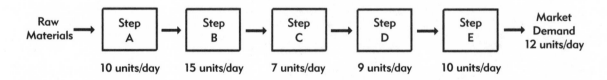

Each of these machines can output a certain number of units per day. The market demands 12 units a day. But the system as it's configured here cannot meet that demand, which suggests one or more bottlenecks.

A bottleneck is any resource whose capacity is equal to or less than the demand placed on it.

According to this definition, it is possible for a system to have more than one bottleneck. However, usually just one of them is the "real constraint." Can you find it?

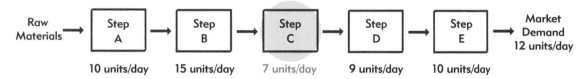

Throughput is 7 units/day **with** Step C **as the constraint**

It should have been fairly straightforward to identify step C as the constraint, because it's the slowest machine.

Step C is also where all attention needs to be placed. Improving the capacity of any other steps is premature optimization. It will have no immediate impact on the overall throughput of the system.

Finding the constraint in this example was easy because I gave you the capacity of each step. This is often not known in advance in a real-world customer factory. So let's rework this problem as you might typically encounter it. This time, all you are able to see are the actual measured output quantities at each step. Can you identify the bottleneck now?

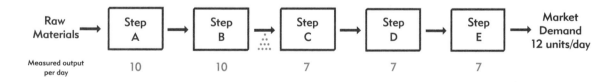

The bottleneck hasn't changed. It is still at step C, but the way you probably spotted it this time was by noticing where the throughput first dipped. The other giveaway of a bottlenecked resource is the piling up of excess inventory in front of it. Because the arrival rate of units at step C (the demand placed on it) is greater than its capacity to process them, this backlog of inventory just keeps growing. This is indicated in the picture above as a heaping pile at step C.

In a customer factory, examples of inventory pileups would be users waiting on you for something—support requests, promised follow-ups, et cetera.

Let's change the problem one more time. Look at the picture below and try to figure out where the bottleneck is now.

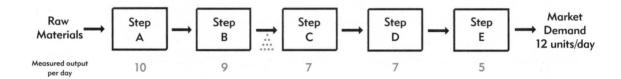

No, the bottleneck still hasn't shifted. Even though step E now outputs the fewest units, it is *not necessarily* the constraint. In this scenario, I introduced the concept of defects (or scrap), which is a practical reality of both real and customer factories. The reason the output of step E dipped is that two of the units passed to it were defective and had to be scrapped.

In our customer factory the concept of defects materializes as users leaving or abandoning one of the steps in the blueprint, which we measure as the conversion rate of that step.

Defects are often caused by mismatched expectations in your positioning, customer segmentation, pricing, solution, et cetera, that cause your users to leave.

Side note: Don't ever call your users defective, or worse, scrap.

While step E's output dropped, what still hasn't changed in the picture above is the heap of inventory at step C—which is the main point of this example.

Excess inventory pileups are the most reliable indicator of bottlenecks—NOT the output level of stages.

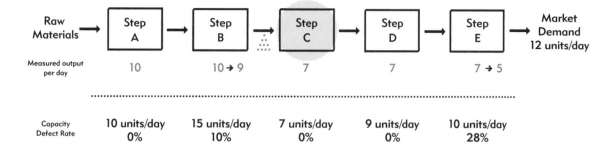

I've redrawn the same scenario, but showing the actual capacities and defect rates so you can see the full picture:

Step C is still the bottleneck here because improving its capacity will improve the throughput of the entire system. This is why it is often also called a capacity constrained resource (CCR).

But What About the Defects?

Sure, reducing the defect rate will also improve throughput and should be a priority. But you have to consider the following factors.

First, we can't readily tell from the picture above if the defect originated at the steps where the defect was detected or further upstream. Further investigation will be needed to get to the root cause. We'll cover techniques for doing this later in the book.

Next, certain types of defects have upper and lower bound limits that are hard to pierce. The theoretical upper limit of a step's conversion rate is 100 percent, but in a typical customer factory it's impossible to get every single person to favorably take the next step with your product. An example of this that I shared earlier was churn rates of SaaS products. At scale, a 2 percent monthly churn is considered healthy. Customers churn for many reasons, and some of these are not "fixable," such as when a customer churns because she successfully completes the job she hired your product to do. Blindly trying to improve your churn rate below a certain threshold will have diminishing and even negative returns on effort.

While reducing defect rates may take extra investigation and/or effort, what should be implemented almost immediately is putting better quality control measures in place right at the bottlenecked step(s). In the example above, defects were detected at two steps—step B and step E—but the value of each is very different.

Defects processed before a bottlenecked step (as at step B) cost us only the value of the raw material. In the case of a customer factory, this maps to the cost of a lead (e.g., the cost of an ad click), which is a small fraction of the overall cost of customer acquisition (COCA). But once these defects reach a bottlenecked step (like step C), the cost of processing defective parts that are subsequently scrapped (as at step E) may mean the cost of a missed sale or, in the case of the customer factory, the lifetime value of a customer. Because step C has a finite processing capacity, it sets the throughput of the entire system. Its time is also the most valuable, and remember that lost time can never be recouped.

Let's apply these concepts to an actual customer factory scenario.

Finding Constraints in a Customer Factory

How do you know where your bottleneck is? Recall the product case study from earlier. Specifically, let's look at the stage where I was delivering my offer through solution interviews with the goal of converting prospects into trials.

In order to do that, I was driving visitors from my blog to a product landing page

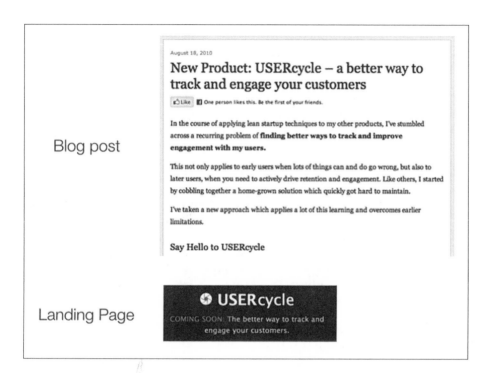

where they could leave their contact information with the expectation of being interviewed (acquisition).

During the interview, I outlined the problems we were addressing, walked them through a demo, and shared our pricing model. This follows the solution interview script outlined in *Running Lean* shown on the next page.

This script has a clear, measurable call to action (CTA) toward the end, which in this case was getting the prospect to provide his credit card and start a trial of our service. In chapter 3, we had estimated the Problem/Solution Fit criteria for this product as establishing a throughput of 30 trials/month, which I've converted below

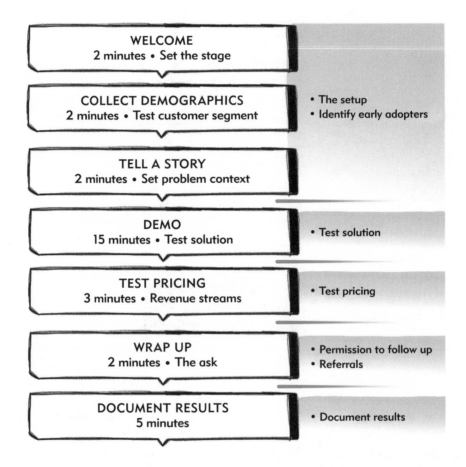

to a weekly rate (to match the timescale of my other steps) shown as the desired throughput goal.

Even though we collected credit card information up front, we didn't actually charge prospects until day thirty, which is why you don't see any realized revenue events in the picture above. You should also notice right away that we are below the goal, which indicates an internal constraint. Here's how you find it:

Week 4: Running Solution Interviews

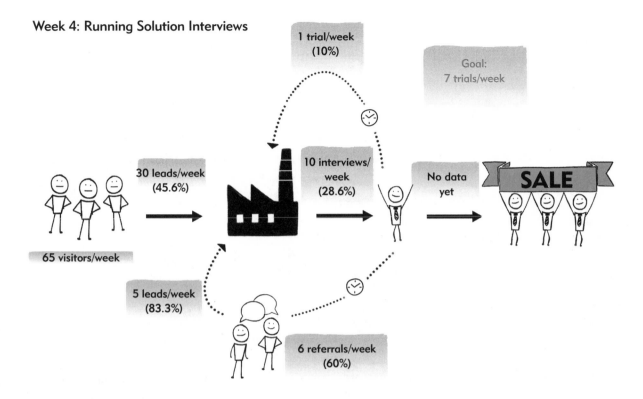

1. FIND BOTTLENECKS

Remember, a bottleneck is where users will be found waiting to be processed. Because a typical landing page can easily handle several thousand visitors per week and because the page itself processes users relatively quickly,* we know there isn't a bottleneck there. We may lose visitors at this step, but that is a conversion issue (due to a defect), not a piling up of inventory.

---

* The time for a visitor to read the page and make a decision is usually on the order of seconds or minutes.

The onboarding process during a trial does take people resources and could potentially be a bottleneck. But at 1 trial/week we weren't hitting any internal capacity issues. Again, no users waiting on us there.

That brings us to the interviewing step. We were taking in 30 leads/week but managing to run only 10 interviews. That means we were dropping 20 leads/week—but from this picture it's not clear if it's because the leads were opting out after learning a little more or because they were waiting on us (inventory pileup). It turned out to be the latter. This was easily witnessed by a growing list of unprocessed leads from one week to the next. While a good problem to have, it is a problem nonetheless. There we have our bottleneck:

Week 4: Running Solution Interviews

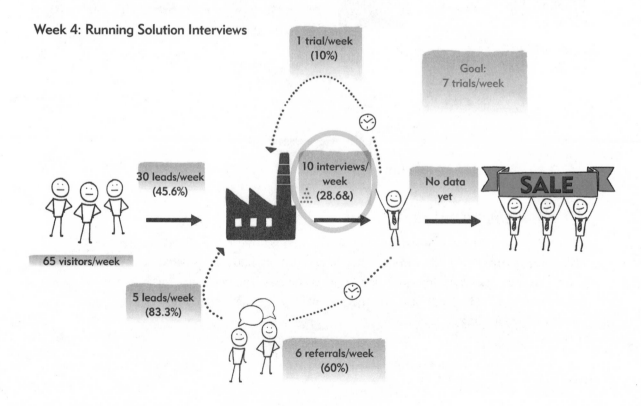

WHAT IF WE HAD BEEN ABLE TO PROCESS ALL THE LEADS COMING IN AND COULDN'T FIND AN INTERNAL BOTTLENECK?

Because the throughput is still below the desired goal, focus would then shift to finding internal defects starting from right to left (highest value to lowest value) and working backward from there.

Had the throughput been at or above the desired goal, the constraint would be outside the system, or a market constraint. The next step would be to drive more traffic and search again for bottlenecks and defects.

2. LIMIT DEFECTS THAT REACH THE BOTTLENECK

You'll notice a big drop-off from interviews to trials, which indicates a defect somewhere in the system. As I pointed out in the last section, defects to the right of the bottleneck (postinterview) are a lot more valuable than defects to the left (preinterview). We don't yet have enough information to identify root causes, but that should be a high priority.

Exercise: How Would You Break This Constraint?

Given what you know about the scenario above, how might you attempt to overcome this constraint?

1. Make a list of three to five action items.
2. Prioritize your list.

Give it some thought before moving on to the next section.

Types of Constraints

Once you've marked potential bottlenecks and/or constraints in your customer factory, the next step is categorizing them. Constraints can be broadly characterized as external or internal constraints, and further subgrouped into physical or policy constraints.

You can probably recognize many of these constraint types. Let's quickly cover them as they map to the customer factory.

Market constraints exist when the demand for a company's products and services is less than the capacity of the organization.

EXTERNAL VERSUS INTERNAL CONSTRAINTS

External constraints, as their name suggests, exist outside the customer factory and are typically market constraints.

The 10x staged rollout strategy actually harnesses this constraint to our advantage. Rather than driving lots of leads into an untested customer factory, we instead limit the intake of new leads in batches defined by our traction model. Only when we can repeatedly process the given batch size of leads with good results do we level up from there.

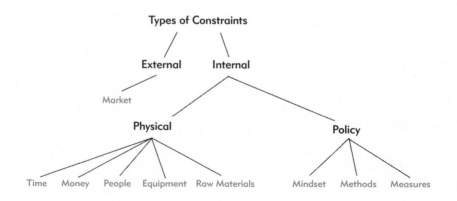

Internal constraints can be further divided into physical constraints and policy constraints.

Physical Constraints

Physical constraints are typically constraints of resources like time, money, or people. We often encounter these resources in limited supply and find ourselves desiring more of them. Ironically, when we have these resources in excess, we become wasteful.

> "When you don't have resources, you become resourceful."
>
> —K. R. SRIDHAR, BLOOM ENERGY

Here are the most commonly encountered physical constraints:

RAW MATERIALS

Raw materials in your customer factory map to unaware visitors entering your factory. These visitors can be acquired from various sources at varying costs of acquisition as described by the channels on the Lean Canvas.

If you follow the 10x launch strategy, you generally don't run into a raw materials constraint during the earlier stages of your product because you can usually find enough starting channels, such as online advertising, social media, and referrals, to get the customer factory going. Over time, though, acquisition of good leads does potentially become a real constraint as you search for scalable and cost-effective channels.

TIME

Of all the resources, time is the scarcest. While all other resources can fluctuate up and down, time moves only in one direction. For this reason, I prioritize it above all other resources.

In the customer factory, we often place a lot of emphasis on conversion rates, but cycle time, or the time it takes to convert a visitor to a customer, is just as powerful a lever.

Consider two viral products with the same conversion rate (viral coefficient) but with two different viral cycle times. The first product has a viral cycle time of two days while the second has a viral cycle time of one day. After twenty days, the first product would have around twenty thousand users while the second could have twenty million users!*

In a B2B scenario, shortening your sales cycle from six months to three months potentially frees up resources to close more accounts faster.

The same idea also applies to your bottlenecked resources. An hour wasted on a bottlenecked resource potentially costs you a lot more than the same hour spent on a nonbottlenecked resource.

MONEY

Money is viewed as a limited resource by most startups. More money lets us upgrade on everything. It lets us hire more people, build more features, and grow. But money is a special kind of resource. It is useful only when it is converted to something else.

If you're building more features or hiring more people but you don't yet know what you are doing, you'll probably just get lost faster. Even when you do know what you are doing, upgrading on all fronts at once risks falling into the local optimization trap. Because each step is highly interconnected, simply optimizing every step does not necessarily lead to higher throughput.

---

* Viral marketing blog post by David Skok: www.forentrepreneurs.com/lessons-learnt-viral-marketing/.

IMVU CASE STUDY

Brett Durrett, CEO of IMVU, gave a presentation at the 2010 Startup Lessons Learned Conference titled "The Evolution of Lean at IMVU."* IMVU is an online 3D avatar chat community and the "original" Lean Startup where Eric Ries cut his teeth on many of the ideas that eventually found their way into *The Lean Startup*.

IMVU had a culture where everyone in the company could test any idea they thought would help the business, which had worked well for them during the early stages of the company. But as IMVU grew its team, this became hard to scale and the company took a dip in revenue.

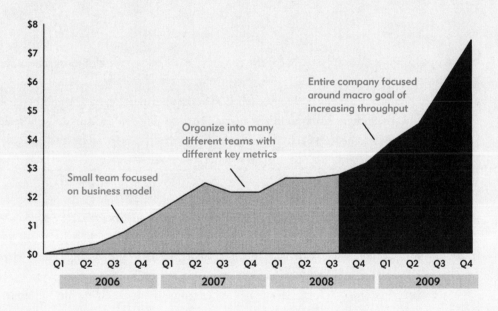

* "The Evolution of Lean at IMVU": www.youtube.com/watch?v=NAw7xK3uGpU.

Its solution was reorganizing the company into many different product groups, each tasked with a single key performance metric to optimize, such as conversion, retention, number of chats, et cetera. Right after this change, IMVU's revenue took a further dip and eventually flatlined. They learned that by organizing their teams around different metrics, they fell into the local optimization trap and actually created a competitive culture that was hurting the company. IMVU's acquisition teams were being rewarded in terms of the number of sign-ups, which were being brute forced by buying lots of cheap traffic. This was not good news for the revenue teams because their conversion rates now plummeted.

By realigning its teams around the bigger macro goal (increasing throughput), IMVU was able to reverse the damage and continue its impressive upward growth trend.

> Money only lets you do more of whatever you are already doing.

For these reasons, it is best to think of money as an accelerant.

From a business model perspective, money can be deployed toward either creating, delivering, or capturing more value. Ultimately, these activities need to be tied back to a net positive return on investment (ROI). In the next chapter, I'll cover how to think through these trade-offs.

EQUIPMENT

Equipment includes things that typically make up a customer factory, such as buildings, servers, and other infrastructure. But it more generally includes things you might build to help turn users into customers, such as your landing pages, copywriting, and features. All these things are part of the overall machinery that makes up your customer factory. Defects in your customer factory technically fall under this category of equipment constraints.

PEOPLE

You need people to build and run your customer factory. Here too, while we often desire more people resources, more isn't always better. With more people on a team you potentially take on more complexity.

When expanding staff, we often end up instituting policies. These policies often start out as best practices. But if we are not careful they can grow into constraints that hold the business back.

> Every process works well until you add people.

Policy Constraints

Policy constraints are typically constraints of habit or ways of thinking, doing, and measuring. It is no coincidence that many apparent physical constraints, upon further analysis, point to one or more of the policy constraints outlined below:

MINDSET

This is a constraint caused by a preexisting way of thinking. Before you can effectively break a constraint, you have to identify the underlying "real constraint," which requires a different way of viewing and tackling your constraints. The next chapter addresses this new way of thinking.

MEASURES

This is a constraint caused by using different—and often conflicting—measures of success. A lot of what we covered earlier in this book addressed this limitation. Before you can make progress, you need a standard measure of progress. The same is true with every new initiative you take on, and you'll see this foundation carry on throughout the rest of the book.

METHODS

This is a constraint caused by preexisting procedures and techniques for carrying out work. When we don't have a way to tie our methods to business results, it is hard to question our methods. A lot of the book thus far has been laying the groundwork for doing just that. In the third part of the book, we're going to cover thinking processes for quickly testing both existing and new methods for getting work done.

Exercise: Identify Your Single Constraint

Take your latest weekly customer factory data and identify potential constraints.

1. Is your customer throughput above your traction goal as described in your traction model?

    If yes, congratulations—you are on track. Your constraint is currently outside the system—a market constraint. Focus on leveling up your throughput by driving more traffic into your customer factory. Then reevaluate your customer factory for bottlenecks and defects again.

    If no, move on to step 2.

2. Do you have an excess inventory, typically a user pileup?

    If yes, these represent bottlenecks in your system. Take a stab at prioritizing the more critical bottleneck or constraint in your system.

    If no, your throughput is most likely limited by one or more defects versus a capacity constrained resource. When searching for defects, look for the biggest drop-offs in conversion rates and the longest processing times. Remember that users create more "potential" value in your system as they move from left to right, so it helps to prioritize your defects in the opposite order.

3. Finally, characterize your constraint into one of the constraint types.

Key Takeaways

- At any given point in time, customer throughput is limited by a single constraint.
- You home in on potential constraints by searching for bottlenecks in your customer factory.
- Bottlenecks are generally where you find excess inventory (like users) piling up.
- Constraints can be internal or external.
- External constraints are market constraints.
- Internal constraints can be broken into physical and policy constraints.
- Starting constraints are usually external.
- Most real constraints are caused by a broken policy.

PART 3
ACHIEVING BREAKTHROUGH

Before you can get to something that works,
you have to go through a lot of stuff that doesn't work.

Goal
Observe and Orient
Learn, Leverage, or Lift
Experiment
Analyze
Next Actions

CHAPTER 7

The Art of the Scientist

AFTER THE INTRODUCTION OF THE SCIENTIFIC METHOD, THERE WAS A marked increase in the pace of breakthrough discoveries. Both science and entrepreneurship operate under conditions of extreme uncertainty, so the thinking goes that the adoption of some entrepreneurial method might do for business innovation what the scientific method did for scientific discoveries: dramatically accelerate the pace. This is the core message of the Lean Startup methodology.

The Scientific Method in a Nutshell

In addition to his contributions to the development of quantum electrodynamics, which won him the Nobel Prize in Physics in 1965, Richard Feynman was recognized as a keen popularizer of the scientific method. He described the scientific method using the following three-step process:

Guess $\longrightarrow$ Compute consequences $\longrightarrow$ Compare to experiment

We start by guessing a new law or a new theory. Then we compute the consequences of our guess. Finally, we compare those computations with experiments or observed experiences.

According to Feynman, this simple statement holds the key to science:

> "If your guess disagrees with experiment, it is wrong. It doesn't matter how beautiful your guess is, how smart you are, who made the guess, or what their name is . . . it is wrong."
>
> —RICHARD FEYNMAN

Guesses Can Only Be Proven Wrong

Another key concept from the scientific method is that guesses or theories can never be proven right— they can only be proven wrong. This is the concept of falsifiability.

Many people don't understand this. They think science is about running experiments to validate our guesses. But you can never run enough experiments to completely validate any guess. All it takes is a single experiment to completely invalidate a guess. In other words, it is possible to formulate a guess, build a model, and run experiments that validate your model. But over time, you might run a wider range of experiments, and gather additional experiences, that no longer agree with your theory and which then prove your theory wrong.

This is what happened to Newton's law for the motion of planets. He guessed the law of gravitation and computed the consequences for the solar system, which matched up with experiments for several hundred years until a slight anomaly was discovered with the motion of Mercury. During all that time, the theory hadn't been proven right, but in the absence of being proven wrong, it was taken to be temporarily right.

This is why true science is hard. The good news is that entrepreneurship is less hard. Entrepreneurs aren't searching for perpetual truths but temporal truths. Our job is to wield these guesses into strategies or growth hacks that make our business model work for some slice of time. These strategies are considered temporarily validated only if they move the business model goal forward—that is, if they result in an increase in throughput. Furthermore, all growth strategies eventually reach saturation when they need to be replaced by new ones.

Even within our current business model trajectory, our "previously validated" guesses can quickly come under question in the face of continuous innovation.

> If you aren't constantly trying to disrupt yourself, i.e., prove your business model wrong, someone else will.

THE PACE OF DISRUPTION IS ACCELERATING

The time slice that we have to work with a given business model has been shrinking. A study conducted by Richard Foster, a professor at Yale University, found that the average life span on the NASDAQ of companies started in the 1920s was a hundred years. By 2010, the average life span had shrunk to just fifteen years.

Toward an Entrepreneurial Method

The closest equivalent to a scientific experiment in innovation is a cycle around the validated learning loop codified by Eric Ries in *The Lean Startup*.

It begins in the "build" stage with a set of ideas or guesses that are used to create some artifact (a mock-up, code, landing page, etc.) for the purpose of testing the idea.

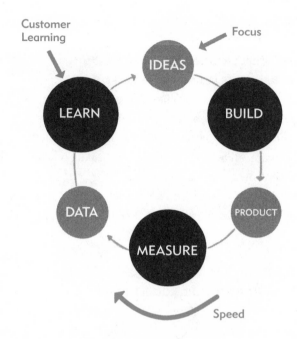

This artifact is used to "measure" customer responses using a combination of qualitative and quantitative techniques for gathering data. This data is then used to derive specific "learning" that either confirms or rejects our guesses. That in turn drives the next set of ideas which inform the next set of actions. Three key attributes for running effective innovation experiments are speed, customer learning, and focus.

However, while experiments are highly effective at testing guesses, simply running experiments is not enough. The output of your experiments can be only as good as the quality of your input guesses. Further, running experiments does not automatically lead to new insights. Many experiments simply invalidate a bad idea and leave you stuck. This begs the question: "Where do good guesses or ideas come from?"

To answer this question, we need to view innovation experiments as part of a larger process of building a repeatable and scalable business model, which we can reword in terms of the goal as:

> Increasing business model throughput while minimizing inventory and operating expenses, provided doing that doesn't degrade throughput.

Here's the three-step entrepreneurial method equivalent for doing this:

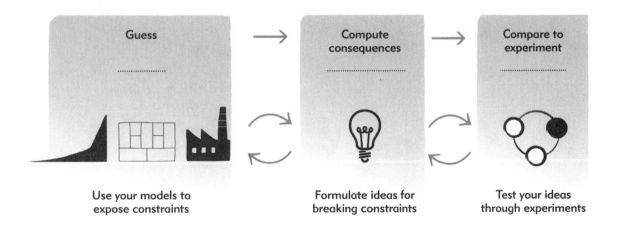

Guess	Compute consequences	Compare to experiment
Use your models to expose constraints	Formulate ideas for breaking constraints	Test your ideas through experiments

1. Use your models to expose constraints.

    Like Einstein's models of the universe, we need simple abstractions to help deconstruct the complex problems of building a repeatable and scalable business.

    The models you have built so far—the Lean Canvas, the traction model, and the customer factory

Good models help expose the right problems to tackle.

blueprint—help describe your business model story, chart your progress, and expose the right constraints to tackle.

2. Formulate ideas for breaking constraints.

With your constraints exposed, you then need to formulate one or more ideas, strategies, or plans for breaking these constraints. Even Lean Thinking, which heavily influenced the Lean Startup, has a deliberate planning step before the build step, which, in our exuberance for action, we failed to emphasize.

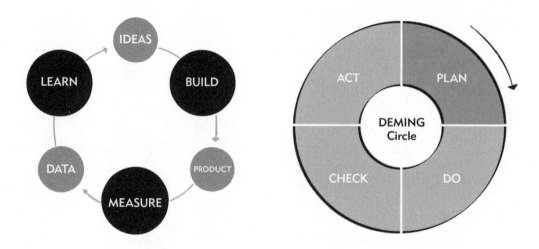

However, like everything else, planning does need to be time boxed to avoid analysis paralysis and force action. But time spent on the right kind of planning is time well spent.

3. Test your ideas through experiments.

These ideas or plans are then tested through one or more small, fast, additive experiments using the Build/Measure/Learn cycle.

We already have the first step of identifying constraints using your models. Let's cover the thinking process for formulating ideas or plans for breaking constraints next.

Breaking Constraints

The word "constraint" evokes a negative feeling in most people. When people face a constraint, they either fall victim and revise their ambition downward, or confront the constraint head-on and look for ways to lift it.

Constraint (noun): something that limits or restricts someone or something.

From a systems perspective, however, constraints are neither good nor bad. Every system always has one, and your business model is no different.

There is a third way to approach constraints:

| To embrace your constraint AND achieve your goal.

This mind shift is the first step toward breaking constraints.

Constraints Create Space for Innovation

In its early days, Southwest Airlines had to sell one of its planes or face bankruptcy. They could have accepted downsizing or knocked on many more investor doors, but instead they asked themselves: "How can we keep our existing routes with three planes instead of four?"

They noticed that the average gate turnaround time for their planes was about sixty minutes. During this time, the plane was cleaned, serviced, and refueled while meals, luggage, and passengers were boarded.

Every minute the plane (bottlenecked resource) spent idle on the ground was valuable. So they looked into ways to reduce this time. They calculated that if they could shrink their gate turnaround times from sixty minutes to ten minutes, they would be able to fly all their current routes with one fewer plane. How do you do this?

Further analysis showed that the passenger boarding process was the biggest contributor to this gate turnaround time. Southwest took on the challenge and introduced a radical new boarding process with no assigned seating. As a result, they managed to keep all their routes with one fewer plane.

But it didn't stop there. Southwest continued to optimize for gate turnaround times even further—ironically, by imposing additional constraints upon itself. While its competitors carried a diverse fleet of planes to support the varying lengths of routes they had to fly, Southwest Airlines made it a policy to fly only a single type of aircraft (Boeing 737s) and fly only short point-to-point routes. A diverse fleet brings with it maintenance complexity, which also contributes to longer gate turnaround times. A single type of aircraft, on the other hand, reduces both the time needed to service a plane and the cost of training mechanics. Other supporting policy constraints that it implemented toward this goal of reducing gate turnaround times were offering only economy seats and no in-flight meals (only peanuts and snacks).

Rather than viewing these constraints as limitations, Southwest Airlines turned them into a differentiated positioning statement: "We are the only short-haul, low-fare, high-frequency, point-to-point carrier in the United States."

Did this differentiation matter? It turned Southwest from an airline on the verge of bankruptcy into one of the most profitable airlines in the industry.

Constraints Are a Gift

Even Facebook's carefully orchestrated staged rollout strategy, which I outlined in chapter 3, didn't start as a well-thought-out strategy but in reaction to a constraint—one of money.

Mark Zuckerberg did not have the money or investors for a full public launch while he was at Harvard. So he limited Facebook's rollout to just three schools: Stanford, Yale, and Columbia. Can you guess what their total monthly spend on servers was at the time? Just $85/month.

Zuckerberg did not want to spend even that amount out of his pocket, so Facebook placed Google AdSense banner ads on their pages, which paid the server hosting bills (and provided early validation for their business model monetization story). Contrast this to today: Facebook spends billions on server hosting every month.

> Before customers can use your product, they have to fire something else—their existing alternatives.

Instead of treating its lack of money as a constraint, Facebook turned it into an opportunity. Stanford, Yale, and Columbia weren't simply three schools chosen at random. They were carefully picked. All three already had vibrant university social networking platforms in place, making them good early adopters. Displacing these existing social networking platforms served to further validate Facebook's unique value proposition.

Additionally, all three were highly respected Ivy League–level universities. A limited staged rollout played up exclusivity and desire, allowing Facebook to position its minimum viable product as a prize that had to be earned by other schools.

How do you apply this kind of thinking to your constraints? That is the topic of the next section.

The Three Focusing Steps

When faced with a constraint, it is tempting to gravitate toward the obvious solution of acquiring more resources to break the constraint. That is often the brute-force approach and usually also the most expensive route.

In his book *The Goal*, Eliyahu Goldratt offers a five-step focusing process for breaking constraints. I have further simplified them into three steps: Learn, Leverage, and Lift.

1. **IDENTIFY** the constraint — Learn what the constraint is

2. **EXPLOIT** the constraint
3. **SUBORDINATE** everything else — Leverage the constraint

4. **ELEVATE** the constraint — Lift the constraint

4. Go back to **STEP 1**

1. LEARN MORE ABOUT THE CONSTRAINT

Before you can break a constraint, you first need to correctly identify it. The steps we covered in the last chapter help you locate a constraint. However, hidden beneath surface constraints there are often deeper constraints that are uncovered only after further analysis. For instance, Southwest Airlines saw through an apparent equipment constraint (number of planes) to a time constraint (gate turnaround time). Solving the latter also fixed the former.

> Correctly identifying the "real" constraint will often drive the right next action you take.

Here are some techniques for doing this:

i. Run a Five Whys analysis.

Five Whys is a question-asking method used to explore the cause/effect relationships underlying a particular problem or undesirable effect. Much like a three-year-old, you take a problem and repeatedly ask: "Why is this a problem?" to surface deeper problems. Unlike a three-year-old, you often don't need to go beyond five levels.

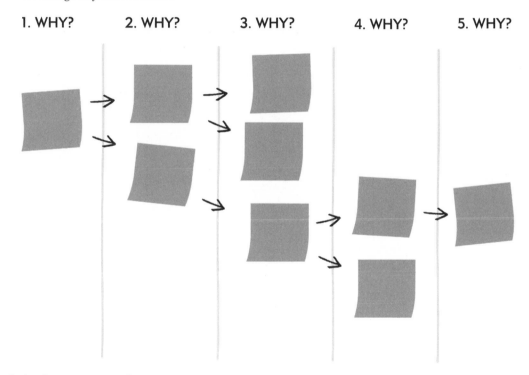

1. WHY?   **2. WHY?**   **3. WHY?**   **4. WHY?**   **5. WHY?**

ii. Analyze your secondary metrics.

While the customer factory dashboard is great for locating the constraint, you often have to drill deeper to uncover potential root causes. Remember that each of the five macro steps in the customer factory blueprint is in turn made up of multiple substeps. After identifying a potential hot spot or constraint, analyzing these substeps can often reveal more specific insights into where and why you are losing users.

Macro metrics help locate where the hot spots lie, while micro metrics help troubleshoot why.

A lot of products, for instance, succeed at getting users signed up, but then users simply leave and never return. We know we have a *retention* problem, but the real challenge is figuring out why. An effective approach is comparing how the behaviors of your users who stay differ from those of users who leave. Yes, this is a kind of cohort analysis. Facebook, for instance, found that users who added at least seven friends in the first ten days were much more likely to stay engaged. It used this insight with great effect to add strategic features that encouraged early friending and grew new user engagement significantly.

iii. Run a learning experiment.

If you still don't have enough information to derive evidence-based root causes for the constraint, the best course of action is running a learning experiment.

WHAT IS A LEARNING EXPERIMENT?

I broadly divide experiments into two categories: Learning experiments and throughput experiments. The end goal of a throughput experiment is increasing traction—unless you run out of potentially good ideas to test. Then you fall back to running learning experiments as a way to generate new ideas (which you then test with one or more throughput experiments).

Learning Experiments
In learning experiments the goal is to uncover potential new insights that become the basis for new guesses or hypotheses. These insights are gathered from customers either

directly through conversation or indirectly through observation.

Here are some examples of learning experiments:

- Problem interviews
- Usability tests
- Surveys

Throughput Experiments

In throughput experiments the goal is to validate (or invalidate) these new insights by way of turning them into measured results; in other words, an increase in one or more of the five traction levers—acquisition, activation, retention, referral, and/or revenue—that subsequently also results in an increase in throughput.

Here are some examples of throughput experiments:

- Solution interviews
- Teaser pages
- A new feature launch

> Learning experiments are for hypothesis generation, while throughput experiments are for hypothesis validation.

After identifying the constraint, the next step is looking for ways to leverage it.

2. LEVERAGE THE CONSTRAINT

You can often find ways of squeezing more efficiencies out of bottlenecked resources or uncovering untapped capacity elsewhere. This step usually requires little to no additional investment of resources and is often enough to break the constraint. This is why leveraging versus lifting a constraint should always be your preferred first course of action.

To avoid the trap of prematurely trying to lift the constraint, it is helpful to ask yourself the following propelling question:*

How can I <achieve the goal> without <acquiring more resources>?

For Southwest Airlines, the propelling question was: "How can we keep our existing routes without acquiring more planes?"

If leveraging the constraint does not end up breaking the constraint, you may then attempt to lift the constraint.

3. LIFT THE CONSTRAINT

Lifting a constraint typically requires improving the capacity of the constrained resource, which almost always also requires some additional investment. This may be an acquisition of additional resources (e.g., equipment, people, leads) or effort spent toward reducing defects (e.g., conversion rates) in the customer factory.

USERcycle Case Study

In the solution interview scenario from chapter 6, we identified the hot spot: losing leads as they were converted into interviews. I was unable to process all the incoming leads, which indicated a resource constraint. The brute-force solution would be assigning more people to run interviews. But does simply throwing more people at the problem address the issue? Not necessarily. Let's see how we can apply the three focusing steps to uncover alternate solutions.

---

* A propelling question is a concept described by Adam Morgan and Mark Barden in their book *A Beautiful Constraint.*

1. LEARN ABOUT THE CONSTRAINT

The first step is exploring possible root causes for the problem beyond the obvious resource constraint, which we did by running a Five Whys analysis.

PROBLEM: Why can't we interview all incoming leads?

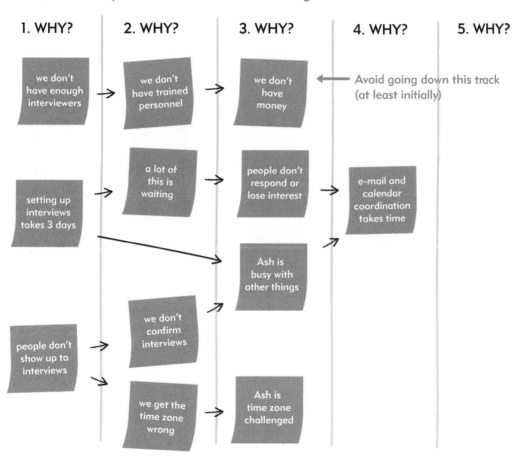

What we learned was that a lot of these interview leads weren't being processed in a timely manner because meeting coordination took effort, I was busy with other things, and I was terrible at this kind of work.

2. LEVERAGE THE CONSTRAINT

The propelling question here is: "How do we process all the interview leads without hiring more people?" The first step is squeezing as much efficiency out of the bottle-necked resource as possible and subordinating everything else to this decision. We started by setting aside predetermined blocks of time for interviews on my calendar and delegating meeting coordination to someone else on the team. That way the bottlenecked resource's time (mine) was never idle and was utilized only toward nondelegable tasks. These two changes alone led to a 50 percent increase. We were now running 15 interviews/week, up from 10 interviews/week.

Staying focused on the overall goal, the real propelling question here is not "How can I run more interviews without adding more interviewers?" but rather "How can I get more trials started without adding more interviewers?"

As we got more interviews under our belt, we ran a different Five Whys analysis—this time to determine why the conversion rate from interviews to trials was so low. Remember that this was a potential defect we identified earlier that we knew would warrant further investigation:

PROBLEM: Why are solution interviews not converting well?

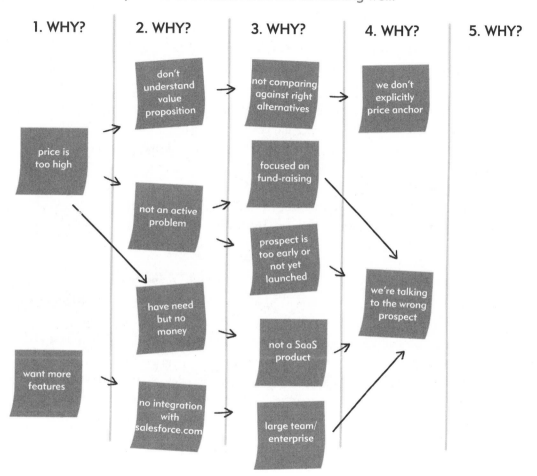

Based on this analysis we identified several reasons why interviews weren't converting. These were the top three:

1. They Did Not Have an Active Problem

A majority of the prospects we interviewed were too early for our solution (some hadn't even launched). While they liked the demo, they were expecting a product in the $0 to $25/month price range—not $200/month. A few other prospects we interviewed were much further along and needed more features to be able to adopt our solution. We ruled out both these groups as outside our ideal early adopter segment.

2. They Had the Problem but No Money

A number of prospects were outside our intended software-as-a-service (SaaS) target, and while they had a similar need, they could not justify the price point because our value proposition did not represent a must-solve problem for them.

3. They Had the Money but Couldn't Justify Our Pricing Model

Others that fit our target criteria were not used to paying more than $100 for third-party services and could not justify the price point to themselves.

I learned all this during the interviews. After you run enough interviews, the principle of repeatability sets in. This is when you can predict the outcome of the interview just by asking a few qualifying questions. I devised three questions that I started asking at the start of the interviews which correlated well enough to whether the prospect signed up. These questions are product specific, but in case you are wondering, they were:

1. How many sign-ups do you get per day?
   Designed to test if there was active need.
2. What is your business model?
   Designed to test if there was early adopter fit.

3. What's keeping you up at night?

Designed to test if goals were aligned.

Our next course of action was administering these questions prior to the interview. Remember that time lost at a bottlenecked resource (my time interviewing noncustomers) is costly and can never be recouped. We did this first over e-mail and later on the interview request page itself. This was a new policy constraint we implemented so that we didn't waste time on noncustomers.

After implementing these changes, these were the measured results:

Week 6: Running Solution Interviews

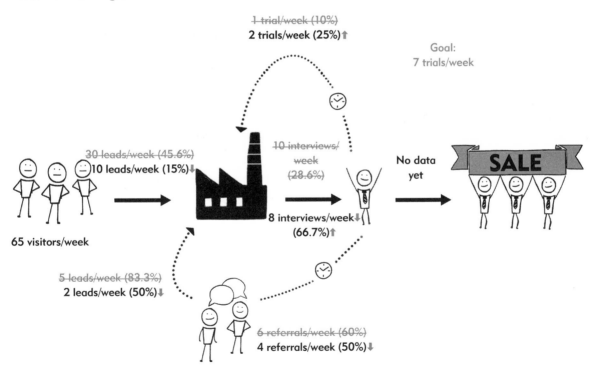

While most of the numbers actually dropped even further, the overall conversion rate to trials more than doubled. This is not an atypical outcome. It highlights the importance of staying focused on the global goal versus local goal(s).

Also notice that the inventory pileup at the interview step is no longer there. The combination of delegating interview coordination and qualifying leads broke this constraint *and* improved overall throughput.

As there is no longer an apparent internal bottleneck, focus then shifted to increasing the number of leads or raw materials entering the factory (market or channels constraint). Additionally, because the throughput remains well under the desired goal, more effort still needed to be expended on identifying defects in the sale process. Further learning from the interviews turned into new hypotheses that were tested in following weeks—like the use of explicit price anchoring during the interview.

Fast-forwarding this story, by week eight we managed to improve our offer enough to achieve an 80 percent conversion rate from interviews to trial and meet our Problem/Solution Fit criteria of starting 30 trials/month.

Where do you capture this type of thinking? Meet the One-Page Validation Plan.

The One-Page Validation Plan

Like the Lean Canvas, the Validation Plan is designed to fit on a single page and be easy to sketch. Also like the Lean Canvas, this is a tool to encourage deep thinking and rapid idea sharing.

This template is based on the A3 report format developed at Toyota, a tool used to solve problems, create plans, and get things done. It is called an A3 report after the international paper size it was designed to fit on. (As the A3 paper size isn't in widespread use anymore, technically the Validation Plan today is an A4 report.)

Embracing the space constraint of a single page forces clarity of your ideas.

The Validation Plan is divided into two halves with a clear delineation down the middle to separate current reality from

VALIDATION PLAN   Title: Author: Created:

Background	Future Reality (The Goal)

Current Condition	Proposal

Analysis	
	Follow-on Plans (if any)

Current Reality   Future Reality

future reality. You read these reports from top to bottom starting with the left-hand side (analysis section), then moving on to the right-hand side (proposal section).

The first thing to establish is the scope of your Validation Plan. Using the journey metaphor, your business model describes your overall vision or destination, which is often years away—making it challenging to formulate an actionable

Validation Plan. A better approach is breaking your overall journey into a set of smaller milestones—no more than three months (or ninety days) into the future. You then formulate a Validation Plan for getting you from wherever you currently are to your next significant milestone.

I'll illustrate this using the USERcycle product and describe a Validation Plan for achieving our first milestone: Problem/Solution Fit.

1. BACKGROUND

You start by briefly describing the business context and importance of a big problem or opportunity you intend to explore.

The backstory of the USERcycle product was that I had already solved some of the problems I described on my Lean Canvas using a homegrown tool I had built for myself. My objective was exploring the viability of turning this homegrown tool into a business model.

2. CURRENT CONDITION

Next you summarize the current situation and highlight the specific problems or constraints currently holding you back. Also highlight any key assets or key resources you might be able to leverage.

In my case, the idea for productizing my homegrown solution came about from conversations during my monthly workshops. I listed these workshops and my blog as possible assets to leverage.

3. ANALYSIS

This is the heart of the analysis and where you apply the first focusing step. Before you can formulate the right strategy for breaking a constraint, you need to correctly identify the "real" constraint.

Because most of my learning for USERcycle had been anecdotal until now, my next action was crafting a learning experiment to gather more insights, which would be followed with throughput experiments to test those insights.

4. FUTURE CONDITION (THE GOAL)

If additional learning is needed, formulate your goal in terms of what you need to learn. Otherwise, formulate your goal as a throughput goal tied to one or more metrics from your customer factory. Finally, make sure to time box your goal. The following fragment helps you to articulate your goals using these guidelines:

Achieve <measurable throughput or learning goal> within <time box>.

Your goals come from your traction model. My goal with the USERcycle product was achieving Problem/Solution Fit for this idea. I time boxed eight weeks for doing this and defined Problem/Solution Fit for my product as getting thirty customer trials started by then. This number comes directly from the traction model we created in chapter 3.

5. PROPOSAL

Next, outline a coarse-grained implementation plan for achieving your goal. This is where you document and classify your idea. Ideas can generally originate from one of the following sources:

I. Root Cause Analysis

These ideas are generally grounded in solid empirical evidence gathered from your Five Whys analysis, data mining, or learning experiments. These proposals typically make the strongest case for pursuing a particular strategy.

II. Other Analogs

These ideas come from examples of strategies that have worked for others. Science is built upon the collective knowledge of many. Innovation is no different.

Sam Walton, best known as the founder of Walmart and Sam's Club, is known to have traveled great distances

> "If I have seen further, it is by standing on the shoulders of giants."
>
> —ISAAC NEWTON

to study his competitors. He would bring back new ideas, like the modern-day centralized supermarket checkout lane, and first try them out in just a few of his stores. If they worked there, he would roll them out to all his stores.

Analogs don't have to come only from rivals. Charles Darwin was heavily influenced by another Charles (Lyell) whose book (*Principles of Geology*) he carried with him on the *Beagle*. Lyell made a case for the gradual evolution of earth through geological processes, which helped Darwin formulate his theory of evolution (which ironically Lyell rejected for many years).

A lot of business model innovation also comes from a remixing of existing patterns across diverse domains. Debundling (music from CDs, TV channels from cable, etc.), disintermediation, and the sharing economy (e.g., Airbnb) are all patterns that have been repeatedly applied across many different domains.

III. Leaps of Faith

Finally, some ideas simply come to us as a hunch or gut feeling. However, as you can probably tell, this is the least defensible type of proposal of the three. The next course of action, though, is still the same if you decide to move forward, is to design a small and fast experiment to test the hunch. We'll cover how to do this in the next chapter.

For the USERcycle product, I decided to use a specific offer type described in *Running Lean* as the "mafia offer." It is called a mafia offer because it's an offer your customers cannot refuse—not because you stronghold them but because it's too good to pass up. You create a mafia offer through a series of problem interviews which help you understand your customers. You deliver a mafia offer through a series of solution interviews to test the offer. I then assigned rough time frames to each activity to meet my eight-week time box.

6. FOLLOW-ON PLANS (IF ANY)

In this section, you outline any next steps you might take if your proposed plan plays out as you expect. This is helpful, for instance, if you had to break down a much bigger strategy to fit into a three-month time box.

After achieving Problem/Solution Fit, my next activities would be packaging my homegrown solution into an MVP and entering the Product/Market Fit stage.

Here's the completed Validation Plan:

VALIDATION PLAN   Title: USERcycle PSFit   Author: Ash Maurya   Created: Aug 1, 2013

Background
I have received several anecdotal requests for turning my homegrown metrics tool into a product, which I want to explore further.

Current Condition
Last 3 workshops with 30 people led to 6 interested parties.

Current Assets:
1. Monthly workshops: 30–40 people
2. Blog: 2,000 unique visitors/week

Analysis
6 interested parties is not yet a problem worth solving. Business model requires 80–100 strong leads.

Leaps of Faith:
1. Problem is active and easy to articulate.
2. Life-cycle messaging solution generates interest.
3. Current channels are sufficient to test PSFit.

Future Reality (The Goal)
Achieve 30 customer trials within 8 weeks.

Proposal
Use interviews to develop mafia offer, then roll out using 10x approach through marketing website.
1. Announce USERcycle with blog post.
2. Drive problem and solution interviews.
3. Develop repeatable offer that works in person.
4. Gradually replace interviews with self-service website.

Time Line:
1. Problem interviews: 2 weeks.
2. Solution interviews: + 4 weeks.
3. Target goal reached: + 2 weeks.

Follow-on Plans (if any)
1. Build MVP
2. Enter Product/Market Fit stage

Exercise: Create a Validation Plan

1. Download and print the Validation Plan template at http://LeanStack.com/validation-plan. You can also create a Validation Plan using the online tool at http://LeanStack.com, but I recommend starting with paper first.
2. Apply the focusing steps to formulate a plan for breaking your constraint and capture it on the one-page template.
3. Share your Validation Plan with someone on your team.

Key Takeaways

- While entrepreneurs can learn from scientists, our goals are different.
- The goal isn't learning but achieving business results—aka traction.
- While running experiments is key, it's not enough.
- The output of your experiments is driven by the quality of your input ideas.
- You source possible solutions by first understanding your problems (constraints) through your models.
- Apply the focusing steps—Learn, Leverage, or Lift—to attempt to break your main constraint.
- Your approach to breaking a constraint can be captured on a One-Page Validation Plan.

CHAPTER 8

Seven Habits for Highly Effective Experiments

THE BEST WAY TO TEST A BIG IDEA OR STRATEGY IS THROUGH SMALL, fast, additive experiments. Because "strategy" is an already overloaded term, let's first start with a definition.

What Is Strategy?

Ask a dozen people what strategy means to them and you'll probably get a dozen different emotionally charged answers, such as this one:

> "Strategy without tactics is the slowest route to victory. Tactics without strategy is the noise before defeat."
>
> —SUN TZU

The term "strategy" first appeared in modern management theory only in the 1960s, but its roots date back to ancient Eastern and Western military philosophy. Since then, a lot has been published on strategic thinking and planning. In 1998, Henry Mintzberg proposed five ways of thinking of strategy:

1. as a plan
2. as a pattern
3. as a perspective
4. as positioning
5. as a ploy

I would argue that while all these definitions seemingly look different, each is a means of achieving a given goal under conditions of uncertainty. The high-level goal of every business is to realize the full potential of a business idea, or more specifically: to build a repeatable and scalable business model. We have seen how to make this goal more concrete by defining it in terms of traction (or throughput). We can use this to offer up a more concise definition of strategy that we use throughout the rest of this book:

> Strategy is a proposal for how to increase customer throughput from point A to point B within a time frame X.

We capture these strategies as ideas that we describe on the One-Page Validation Plan we covered in the last chapter.

Testing Big Strategies Through Small Experiments

There is a natural tension between keeping experiments small and fast and achieving breakthrough insights. Business model breakthroughs are usually associated with grand strategies that take time to implement. But you can always test a grand strategy by scoping down and first testing for lower-level signals or leading indicators.

For instance, if you wanted to test a new content marketing strategy, what would you do? Here's a possible task list:

1. Pick a name for your blog.
2. Register a domain.
3. Design a logo.
4. Set up a WordPress site.
5. Publish your first blog post.
6. Promote the blog post.

The first four items on this list require acquisition of additional resources. While relatively inexpensive in money terms, they cost time, which is more valuable than money. More important, they don't do much to test the riskiest assumption in this strategy, which is "Can you write compelling content that engages your audience?" This is tested only in steps 5 and 6.

Do you even need your own blog to do this? You can instead leverage other people's networks by guest blogging first. Not only does it get you to step 5 faster, it also takes care of step 6.

So what do you need to secure a guest blog post? You don't need to write a full blog post at first. What if it isn't what the blogger wants for his audience?

Here's a much faster way to test this strategy:

1. Find the "right" bloggers who overlap with your audience.
2. Contact them with a few titles and excerpts of possible blog posts that work for their audience (and you, of course).
3. If one or more of them bite, then write the blog post.
4. Link back to your own landing page at the bottom of your post.

Not only is this experiment much faster to run than the first approach, but it tests for the right lower-level signals early. If your guest blog post fails to engage your audience, why would you invest in this strategy? If, on the other hand, the guest blog post is well received, you could write more guest blog posts, and even start investing in creating your own branded blog.

If you noticed, I used the three focusing steps—Learn, Leverage, Lift—to come up with the validation strategy above. Instead of rushing to start a blog site, the propelling question in my head was: "How can I test content marketing without creating my own blog?"

Every time you release a new feature, run a marketing campaign, or try a new sales method, you are testing a new strategy using some kind of experiment. The real question isn't whether you run experiments, but rather whether you run good experiments. This chapter will outline the ground rules for designing and running good experiments.

A single experiment can never completely validate a strategy, but it can completely invalidate it.

Cognitive Biases

Cognitive biases affect our decision-making ability. Even celebrated scientists like Isaac Newton weren't immune to these biases.* For this reason, the scientific community has built-in procedures and safeguards for how empirical research is conducted and how evidence is gathered.

> "The first principle is that you must not fool yourself and you are the easiest person to fool."
>
> —RICHARD FEYNMAN

During clinical trials for medicinal drug testing, for instance, researchers go to great lengths to set up double-blind tests where information about the test is kept from both the testers and the subjects until afterward.

However, conducting entrepreneurial inquiry at this

---

* Researchers have found that Newton fudged some of the numbers in his *Principia*, considered the greatest treatise on physics ever written.

level of rigor can be overkill. Entrepreneurship isn't knowledge acquisition for learning's sake, but for the sake of driving results. Our goal, as entrepreneurs, is to quickly latch on to the right signal in the noise and then double down on the signal.

Testing a few gut-based shortcuts (or hunches) along the way is sometimes the fastest way to find these signals in the noise. What follows is a condensed list of seven habits that will help you counteract your cognitive biases while testing your hunches.

1. DECLARE YOUR EXPECTED OUTCOMES UP FRONT

Much as a scientist doesn't simply go into the lab and start mixing a bunch of compounds to "see what happens," you can't go into an experiment without having an idea of what you're looking for.

Here's how this bias creeps up on us: Say you launch a product in the summer months and it doesn't sell—it's obviously because everyone is on vacation. If your product still doesn't sell in the fall, it's probably because everyone just came back from vacation—and they're not yet ready to buy. Then here in the United States, at least, we have Halloween, Thanksgiving, and Christmas, all of which conspire to drive down your sales. By this logic, it's never a good time to sell anything.

Instead of falling into this kind of postrationalization trap, you need to take a more empirical approach. Instead of simply waiting to see what happens, you need to declare your expected outcomes up front—and factor in things like seasonality. This is more easily said than done. There are usually two deeper reasons for not wanting to declare outcomes up front:

> "If you simply plan on seeing what happens you will always succeed at seeing what happens because something is guaranteed to happen."
>
> —ERIC RIES, *THE LEAN STARTUP*

> Reasonably smart people can rationalize anything, but entrepreneurs are especially gifted at this.

i. We hate to be proven wrong.
ii. It's hard to make educated guesses about the unknown.

The next two habits overcome these objections.

2. MAKE DECLARING OUTCOMES A TEAM SPORT

If you are the founder or CEO of a company, you might shy away from making bold public declarations of expected outcomes because you want to appear knowledgeable and in control. You don't even have to be the CEO to exhibit this behavior. If you are a designer proposing a new design, it's much safer to be vague on results than to declare a specific lift in conversion rates for fear of being proven wrong.

The underlying reason most people shy away from up-front declarations is that we attach our egos to our work. While egos are good for reinforcing ownership, they are bad for empirical learning.

I know it's not easy to consciously detach your ego from your product. After all, you probably spend most of your waking hours working on your product. I reached a point in my entrepreneurial journey where it became more important to build the right product than to always be right. This mind shift is essential to building a healthy culture of experimentation.

You can show your fear of declaring outcomes in another way: by making only safe declarations. You don't achieve breakthroughs by taking the safe route. You need to develop a culture that allows people to have strong opinions, strange hunches, and weird instincts that they can then rigorously test.

STRONG OPINIONS, WEAKLY HELD

People so hate to be proven wrong that in crucial decision-making moments, they'll take the safe or neutral route.

> Or they'll fall into an endless analysis/paralysis cycle.
> Waiting for that perfect piece of information.
> But there is a slim chance for achieving breakthrough

when you're just nodding your head all the time,
or drowning in a sea of nonactionable data.
Breakthrough comes from taking a different stance,
a different perspective. A different approach.
Sure, you'll probably be wrong most of the time.
But if you never stick your neck out,
you guarantee you'll never be right even once
on something that really matters.

Here's how I propose you get started. Don't place the burden of declaring expected outcomes on a single person. Instead, make it a team effort, but with a twist.

Seeking team consensus too early can lead to groupthink. Expected outcome declarations are particularly vulnerable to being influenced by the HiPPOs in the room.

It's much better instead to have team members declare outcomes individually first and then compare notes.

So in the case of a designer proposing a new landing page, for instance, the designer would first walk the team through her proposal. Then everyone on the team esti-

HiPPO is an acronym used at Amazon which stands for the "highest-paid person's opinion."

mates the potential throughput lift in conversion rate independently. After their estimates are in, they then compare their estimates and discuss how they arrived at those numbers.

I recommend having a similar officewide poll after running an experiment and after the actual results have come in. If you want to have a little fun, you can turn this exercise into a game where you award a small token prize to the person with the closest estimate.

The point isn't about being right or wrong but about getting your team comfortable with declaring expected outcomes. This exercise alone can dramatically help improve your team's judgment over time.

If you are a solo founder, it's even more important to write down your expected outcomes before running experiments.

3. EMPHASIZE ESTIMATION, NOT PRECISION

The other reason people shy away from declaring expected outcomes up front is that they feel they don't have enough information to make meaningful predictions. If you've never launched an iPhone app before, how can you possibly predict an expected download rate?

Here are three ways to do this:

You need to accept the fact that you will never have perfect information AND that you need to make these kinds of predictions anyway.

I. Search for Analogs

In an ideal world, we would be able to look up the expected conversion rates on any metric. Most companies, however, choose to keep the internal workings of their customer factory secret for competitive reasons. Some of these numbers can be pieced together with a little research, as we did in the business model ballparking exercise from chapter 2.

However, the most accurate estimates will come through investing in improving your own judgment over time. You have to become an expert on your own customers' behavior patterns. The only way to do this is to declare outcomes up front and incrementally learn from each outcome.

When you first start declaring these outcomes, be prepared for these numbers to be way off. For instance, you might expect to get 100 downloads per day from your iPhone app launch, but you find that you get only 10 downloads per day. Your first guess may have been overly optimistic, but when you are consistently off by a magnitude of 10, you naturally start adjusting your expectations to match reality.

II. Use Your Traction and Customer Factory Models

It's important to keep in mind that you don't simply pick numbers, like 100 downloads per day, out of thin air. These numbers should come from your traction and customer factory models. The point of building a model in the first place is that you use it to predict how your customers need to behave to make your business work (compute consequences), which you then validate or invalidate through experiment.

III. Start with Ranges Instead of Absolute Predictions

Most people also shy away from making any predictions at all because they feel the need to be exact.

Here is another estimation technique by way of Douglas Hubbard. It builds on research that shows that assessing uncertainty is a general skill that can be taught with measurable improvement. His technique is built on making predictions in ranges rather than in absolutes. He illustrates this technique with an estimation exercise that I have used quite effectively in my workshops.

> Any estimation is better than no estimation.

Exercise: What Is the Wingspan of a Boeing 747 Airplane?

Unless you are in aviation, you probably throw your hands up in the air when faced with a question like this one. Instead of attempting a single answer, you can break the problem into two by first tackling the upper bound to a 90 percent confidence interval and then doing the same with the lower bound. Let's give it a try.

CAN THE WINGSPAN BE LESS THAN 20 FEET (6 METERS)?

No, that would obviously be too short.

We are 100 percent certain of this.

How about 30 feet (9 meters)?

Keep increasing this number until you are no longer comfortable going any higher. You should be aiming for 90 percent certainty.

Write this number down. Then repeat for the upper bound.

CAN THE WINGSPAN BE GREATER THAN 500 FEET (152 METERS)?

No, that would obviously be too long.

We are also 100 percent certain of this.

How about 300 feet (91 meters)? That's the length of a football field.

Keep decreasing this number until you are no longer comfortable going any lower. Again aim for 90 percent certainty and write this number down.

HOW DID YOU DO?

The correct answer is 211 feet (64 meters).

When I've run this exercise in my workshops, students have gone from declaring they don't know the answer to hitting a range within 5 to 20 feet of the right answer!

You can apply this same technique to your throughput experiments. The lower and upper bounds of conversion rates already have set floors and ceilings. Let's take the acquisition or sign-up rate as an example. We know it can't be 100 percent—no one gets that. And it can't be 0 percent—there would be no point to the experiment. Through progressive adjusting of your lower and upper bounds, you might create a 90 percent confidence interval of a 20 to 40 percent sign-up rate.

That's progress. Over time, your confidence will go up and your ranges will shrink.

4. MEASURE ACTIONS VERSUS WORDS

All throughput experiments need to define expected outcomes in terms of one or more customer factory actions. Learning experiments, however, can be a bit more challenging because qualitative learning can be subjective. Ask any entrepreneur how a customer call went and it's usually all positive. This is confirmation bias at work, where we tend to selectively retain only that which agrees with our preexisting worldview and ignore the rest. Rather than trying to qualitatively gauge what users say, measure what they do (or did).

Let's take problem interviews as an example. Problem interviews, as described in *Running Lean*, are carefully scripted customer conversations with an objective of

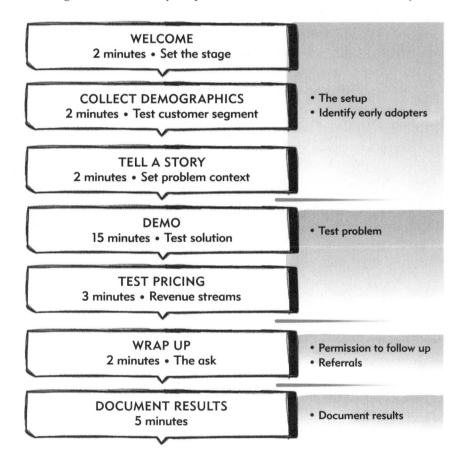

learning about your customers' problems. If you simply seek validation to a list of problems, you'll get poor results because people lie—either out of politeness, ignorance, or to avoid confrontation. In these interviews, it is critical to first set the context around the problems you want to explore, but then to ask open-ended questions. Your objective is seeking confirmation of what people might have declared as fact (like their ranking of problems) from past actions. So rather than asking a leading question like "Will you use X to solve problem Y?," ask them instead, "Tell me the last time you encountered problem Y and how did you solve it?"

Similarly, every learning experiment should end with a clear, measurable call to action, even if that action is a microcommitment, like permission to follow up or a referral to someone else. These are usually placed toward the end of the interview.

If you wasted thirty minutes of a prospect's time in an interview, while he might be polite, he will not pay you with more of his time in a follow-up or burn his social capital by referring you to others. These types of microcommitments serve as measurable user actions that help confirm what people say against what they do.

5. TURN YOUR ASSUMPTIONS INTO FALSIFIABLE HYPOTHESES

Next, it's not enough to simply declare outcomes up front. You have to make them falsifiable or capable of being proven wrong. I touched on this earlier when discussing the scientific method.

It is extremely difficult to invalidate a vague theory.

Falsifiability is required to avoid falling into the inductivist trap, where we gather just enough information to convince ourselves that we are right. You might already be familiar with this trap from the famous white swans example. If all the swans you've ever seen are white, it's easy to declare that all swans are white. But it takes only one black swan to disprove this theory.

Let's see how this problem surfaces with a business model assumption stated as "I believe that my being considered an expert will drive early adopters to my product."

To test this statement, you might mention your product in talks, tweet a link, or write a blog post. All of these things may start driving sign-ups. But when do you declare this statement as validated? Is it when you get 10 sign-ups, 100 sign-ups, or 1,000 sign-ups? The expected outcome is vague.

The other problem with this approach is that when you mix a bunch of activities together, it is hard to draw lines between activities and causality. Can your sign-ups really be attributed to all these activities equally, or is there one driving most of the sign-ups?

The statement above is a good first pass at a "leap of faith" but it isn't yet a falsifiable hypothesis. It needs to be refined further so that it's more specific and testable. Here's a much better version:

| Writing a blog post will drive >100 sign-ups.

Now we have a way of running this experiment and clearly measuring whether it passes or fails. Remember from the last section that this 100 sign-ups number isn't simply pulled out of thin air—it needs to be derived from your traction and customer factory models.

The key takeaway here is realizing that assumptions on your canvas generally don't start out as falsifiable hypotheses but as leaps of faith. In order to turn leaps of faith into falsifiable hypotheses, you rewrite them as:

| <Specific Testable Action> will drive
| <Expected Measurable Outcome>.

So far we have covered two habits for crafting an effective experiment: declaring outcomes up front and making them falsifiable. But that's not enough. There's still something missing in the expected outcome statement above. Can you figure out what it is?

6. TIME BOX YOUR EXPERIMENTS

Say you run the experiment and decide to check back in a week. After a week, you have 20 sign-ups. You might decide it's a good start and leave the experiment running for another week. Now you have 50 sign-ups, which is right at the halfway point of your desired goal of 100 sign-ups. What should you do?

> Just as the inductivist trap allows us to declare success prematurely, lacking a time box allows us to indefinitely extend our experiments.

Entrepreneurs, being overly optimistic, commonly fall into the trap of running the experiment "just a little while longer" in the hopes of getting better results. The problem here is that when the experiment is left to run unchecked, those weeks easily turn into months.

Remember that time—not money or people—is the scarcest resource we have. The solution is time boxing your experiment. We can then rewrite the expected outcome as:

> Writing a blog post will drive >100 sign-ups in two weeks.

Setting a time box like this sets up a nonnegotiable trip wire for a future discussion with your team irrespective of the results—provided, of course, that the world doesn't come to an end.

I recommend going even one step further with time boxing. Rather than trying to estimate how long it will take to run a particular type of experiment, constrain all your experiments to fit within the same time-box interval.

In other words, all your experiments need to fit within a predefined time box, irrespective of type. It is perfectly okay to revise the goal downward to fit your time box. For instance, in the example from earlier, if you don't think you can hit 100 sign-ups in two weeks, but you can do it in four weeks, split it into two experiments:

Experiment 1:

Writing a blog post will drive >50 sign-ups in the first two weeks.

Experiment 2:

The blog post will drive >50 sign-ups in the next two weeks.

If after the first two-week experiment you have only 10 sign-ups, you'll know that there's a low likelihood of making it up in the next two weeks unless you take some corrective action. Think of time boxing as a way to force smaller batch sizes in your experiments. The smaller the batch, the faster the feedback loop from the experiment.

I've applied this time constraint technique in both small and large teams with equal efficacy. Before a time-box constraint was imposed, the teams were scoping their experiments from a couple of weeks for small experiments to several months for large experiments. On the longer experiments, the only visibility on progress was the team's build velocity, which, as we established earlier, is an unreliable progress indicator.

We then instituted a two-week time box and prescheduled progress update meetings with project overseers. This meant that the team had to find a way to build, measure, learn, and be prepared to communicate business results every two weeks.

Like magic, the team stepped up. They found creative ways of breaking up their "big" experiments into smaller experiments. Through these faster feedback loops, they were able to invalidate several large initiatives early and generate more confidence on others. Both these outcomes are progress.

7. ALWAYS USE A CONTROL GROUP

Progress is relative. In order to tell if an experiment is working, you need to be able to benchmark it against a previous state. The equivalent in science would be establishing a control group.

Your daily, monthly, and weekly customer factory batches are a reasonable starting point for establishing a control baseline. These time-based batches create a benchmark that you should aim to beat in your experiments. This is a kind of serial split testing, and it's usually acceptable when you either don't yet have a lot of users or aren't running simultaneous overlapping experiments.

That said, the gold standard for creating a control group is through parallel split testing. In parallel split testing you expose only a select subgroup of your user population to an experiment. Then compare group A with the rest of the population (control group) to determine progress (or not). This is also called an A/B test.

Finally, if you have enough traffic to test with and more than one possible conflicting solution to test, you can run an A/B/C (or more) test where you pit multiple ideas against one another.

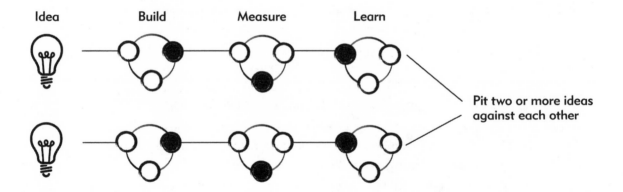

Idea   Build   Measure   Learn

Pit two or more ideas against each other

The One-Page Experiment Report

Like the One-Page Validation Plan, there is also a One-Page Experiment Report. Instead of your having to memorize these seven habits, the Experiment Report incorporates them and functions both like a checklist and an idea-sharing tool.

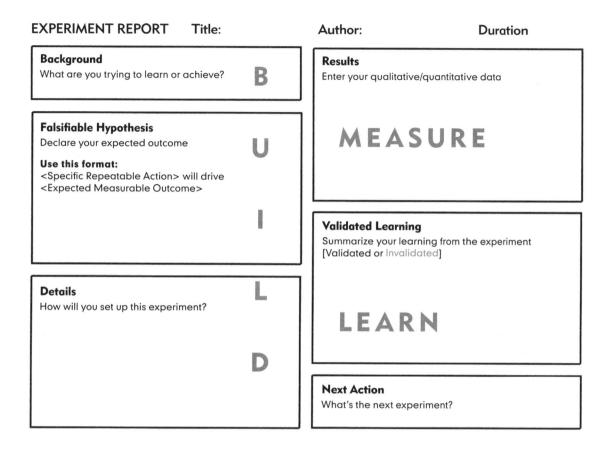

EXPERIMENT REPORT   Title: Author: Duration

Background
What are you trying to learn or achieve?

B

Falsifiable Hypothesis
Declare your expected outcome

Use this format:
<Specific Repeatable Action> will drive
<Expected Measurable Outcome>

U

I

Details
How will you set up this experiment?

L

D

Results
Enter your qualitative/quantitative data

MEASURE

Validated Learning
Summarize your learning from the experiment
[Validated or Invalidated]

LEARN

Next Action
What's the next experiment?

Unlike with the Validation Plan, you don't fill out this report all at once, but in stages, following the build-measure-learn cycle of experiments.

Here are the steps for filling out an Experiment Report. First, pick a suitable action-driven name for your experiment—for example, "Run Problem Interviews" or "Test Landing Page." Next, pick a suitable time box for your experiment. If unsure, start with two weeks.

I'll illustrate this process by building upon the Validation Plan for the USERcycle product from the last chapter. My next task was defining the first experiment.

BUILD

1. Background

Start by outlining the high-level goal of this experiment as it relates to the overall Validation Plan you are testing. In my case, my objective was to use a teaser page plus a blog post to drive interview leads, which was the first step in the implementation plan.

2. Falsifiable Hypotheses

Next you need to declare your outcomes up front while making them falsifiable. Convert all your leaps of faith into falsifiable hypotheses using the fragment:

> \<Specific Repeatable Action\> will drive
> \<Expected Measurable Outcomes\>.

I worded my falsifiable hypothesis as:
"Teaser page + blog post will collect >100 interview leads."

3. Details

The details section is where you outline the specifics of your experiment. You might include things like:

- What will you build?
- How will you measure results?
- What resources do you need?
- How long will it take?

That's all you need to define the experiment and share it with your team.

USERcycle Case Study

EXPERIMENT REPORT   Title: Find interview prospects   Author: Ash Maurya   Duration: 2 weeks

Background
Use teaser page + blog post to drive interview leads for the USERcycle product.

Results

Falsifiable Hypothesis
1. Teaser page + blog post will collect >100 interview leads.

Rationale:
• Expected blog post traffic: 2,000 visitors
• Expected conversion rate: 10%
• Expected interview leads: 200

Validated Learning

Details
1. Announce USERcycle product through a blog post.
2. CTA is to drive interested parties to teaser page with expectation of being interviewed.
3. Use Google Analytics and Prefinery to measure conversion rates.

Next Action

If you decide to move forward with your experiment, your next steps will be building out the experiment. As soon as the experiment is built and launched, you start collecting data and enter the measure stage.

Exercise: Define an Experiment

1. Download and print the Experiment Report template at http://LeanStack .com/experiment-report. You can also create an Experiment Report using the online tool at http://LeanStack.com, but I recommend starting with paper first.

2. Using the Validation Plan you created in the last chapter, fill out the Build section of the Experiment Report.

3. Share your Experiment Report with someone on your team.

MEASURE

During the experiment, you collect data using the appropriate tool for the job. This may be a set of online analytics tools or something more manual. An experiment is marked complete when one of three things happens:

1. You Satisfy All the Expected Outcomes

This is when you meet or exceed your declared outcomes before the experiment time box. Instead of waiting, you can mark the experiment as validated and move on to decide the next action.

2. The Time Box for the Experiment Expires

Once the time box expires, even if you are close to meeting your declared outcomes, you don't extend the time box but rather record your latest results and mark the experiment complete.

3. Something Bad Happens

Once in a while you might run an experiment that does a lot more harm than good. You might, for instance, roll out a feature or raise prices in such a way that it creates an immediate user uproar. In these instances, it may not be prudent to wait the full time box. You might instead record your learning and mark the experiment complete to limit the damage.

At the end of the experiment, you summarize your findings in the Results box on the Experiment Report using the following format:

> \<Specific Repeatable Action\> resulted in
> \<Actual Measured Outcomes\>.

Notice how it's worded. This format makes it easy to compare your actual results against your expected outcomes.

USERcycle Case Study

EXPERIMENT REPORT   **Title: Find interview prospects**   **Author: Ash Maurya**   **Duration: 2 weeks**

Background

Use teaser page + blog post to drive interview leads for the USERcycle product.

Falsifiable Hypothesis

1. Teaser page + blog post will collect > 100 interview leads.

Rationale:
- Expected blog post traffic: 2,000 visitors
- Expected conversion rate: 10%
- Expected interview leads: 200

Details

1. Announce USERcycle product through a blog post.
2. CTA is to drive interested parties to teaser page with expectation of being interviewed.
3. Use Google Analytics and Prefinery to measure conversion rates.

Results

1. Teaser page + blog post campaign resulted in 134 interview leads.

Validated Learning

Next Action

LEARN

While your measured results are intended to be fact based, the Validated Learning section on the Experiment Report is where you attempt to interpret these results.

If the experiment validated your expected outcomes, you can pat yourself on the back and go on to define the next additive experiment that moves your strategy validation forward.

EXPERIMENT REPORT   Title: Find interview prospects   Author: Ash Maurya   Duration: 2 weeks

Background
Use teaser page + blog post to drive interview leads for the USERcycle product.

Falsifiable Hypothesis
1. Teaser page + blog post will collect > 100 interview leads.

Rationale:
• Expected blog post traffic: 2,000 visitors
• Expected conversion rate: 10%
• Expected interview leads: 200

Details
1. Announce USERcycle product through a blog post.
2. CTA is to drive interested parties to teaser page with expectation of being interviewed.
3. Use Google Analytics and Prefinery to measure conversion rates.

Results
1. Teaser page + blog post campaign resulted in 134 interview leads.

Validated Learning
This number was lower than the projected outcome but enough to complete Problem/Solution Fit stage.

An interesting number to note is the 45.6% conversion rate on the application form. The blog post drove traffic to the page, but slightly less than half completed the form.

The rest were either just curious or didn't completely read the blog post?

Next Action
Continue running problem interviews.

If, however, the experiment fails to validate your expected outcomes, what you do next is even more important and the topic of the next chapter.

TPS REPORTS

When I first introduced the One-Page Validation Plans and Experiment Reports to my team, they were met with resistance and even compared to filling out the useless TPS reports from Mike Judge's cult-classic movie *Office Space*. I'll come out and admit up front that I'm not big on process and even have an inner aversion to it. Like many of you, I've worked at large companies and lived through many needless "TPS reports." But at Toyota they view their TPS (Toyota Production System) reports differently.

> "The right process will produce the right results."
>
> —JEFFREY LIKER, *THE TOYOTA WAY*

A process is not something mandated from the top and set in stone, but should rather be a living product that is owned by the people doing the work. When we started, these one-page reports did not look like they do today. They are the product of hundreds of hours of tweaking, testing, and iterating. Here are the top three benefits we continue to derive from them:

1. They crystallize our thinking and shorten meeting times.

    While your ideas might be clear in your mind, you realize how fuzzy they are only once you put them down in writing and share them with someone else. We used to spend many hours in meetings each week trying to understand one another's ideas. By using these one-page reports as a checklist, we now get to clearer ideas faster and spend more time pushing ideas forward.

2. They create a learning archive so you don't forget what you did.

    If you run a lot of experiments, as we do, you eventually start forgetting the results of things you previously tested. We have had to rerun several tests because we never archived the results. At Toyota, they treat their A3 reports as a company knowledge archive. Every car ever built has a binder with copies of these reports that are made available to everyone in the company.

3. They help with onboarding new team members so you get to work faster.

Whenever we add a new member to the team or speak with an adviser, they are highly motivated to help and come up with lots of ideas. The problem is that we have usually already tried most of them. We now instead point them to an online repository of our reports and have them review the last sixty days' worth of ideas and experiments. The result is much more productive conversations.

In chapter 11, I'll share how you can use these reports to tell an effective business model progress story to your stakeholders.

Key Takeaways

- Every grand strategy can be tested with one or more small, fast, additive experiments.
- Internalize the seven habits for running highly effective experiments:
    1. Declare your expected outcomes up front.
    2. Make declaring outcomes a team sport.
    3. Emphasize estimation, not precision.
    4. Measure actions rather than words.
    5. Turn your assumptions into falsifiable hypotheses.
    6. Time box your experiments.
    7. Always use a control group.
- Capture your experiments on a One-Page Experiment Report.

CHAPTER 9

Dealing with Failure

CAN YOU FIND THE COMMON THEME ACROSS THESE DISCOVERIES: PENIcillin, microwave, X-ray, gunpowder, plastics, and vulcanized rubber?

Yes, they were all accidental discoveries. But because they were accidental, it's easy to dismiss them as lucky breaks. However, there was more than luck at play. All these discoveries started as failed experiments.

In each of these cases, the inventors were seeking a specific outcome and instead got a different outcome. But instead of throwing away their "failed" experiments, they did something very different from most people: they asked why.

Innovation experiments are no different. Achieving breakthrough, then, is less about luck and more about a rigorous search. The reason the hockey-stick trajectory has a long flat portion in the beginning is not because the founders are lazy and not working hard, but because before you can find a business model that works, you have to go through lots of stuff that doesn't.

> Breakthrough insights are often hidden within failed experiments.

Most entrepreneurs, however, run away from failure. At the first sign of failure, they rush to course correct *without taking the requisite time to dig deeper and get to the root cause of the failure*. In the Lean Startup methodology, the term "pivot" is often used to justify this kind of course correction. But this, of course, is a misuse of the term:

A pivot not grounded in learning is simply a disguised "see what sticks" strategy.

The key to breakthrough isn't running away from failure but, like the inventors above, digging in your heels and asking why. The "fail fast" meme is commonly used to reinforce this sentiment. But I've found that the taboo of failure runs so deep (everywhere except maybe in Silicon Valley) that "failing fast" is not enough to get people to accept failure as a prerequisite to achieving breakthrough. You need to completely remove the word "failure" from your vocabulary.

There is no such thing as a failed experiment, only experiments with unexpected outcomes.

—BUCKMINSTER FULLER

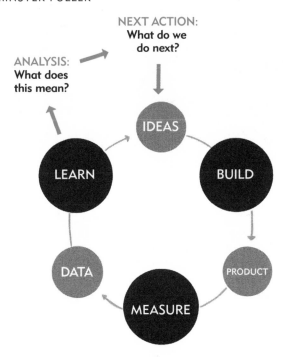

Try to see so-called failures as instances where your model of customer behavior did not match your observed experience. In these instances, you need to either try a different approach or revise your model. Just as the quality of your input ideas drives your results, the quality of your postexperiment analyses drives your next breakthrough insights.

Analyze Your Results

The **Analyze** step in the GO LEAN framework is where you attempt to reconcile your observed results with your expected outcomes. Your results provide a feedback loop that you process in reverse—first at the experiment level, then at the strategy or Validation Plan level, and finally in your models.

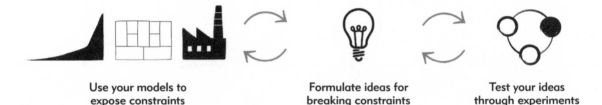

Use your models to expose constraints   Formulate ideas for breaking constraints   Test your ideas through experiments

1. ANALYZE YOUR EXPERIMENT

If your observed results match up against your expected outcome, you can pat yourself on the back and move to the next step of analyzing your Validation Plan against the goal.

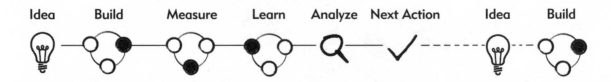

Idea   Build   Measure   Learn   Analyze   Next Action   Idea   Build

If, however, you were pitting two (or more) different approaches as competing experiments (an A/B test), it is possible that experiments from each yield positive results, but you can't keep both approaches. You need to declare a winner.

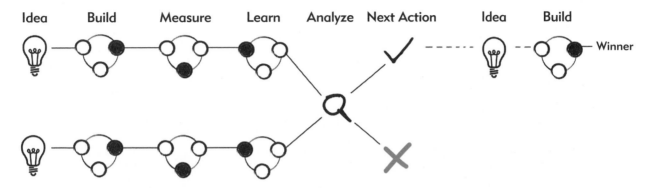

If, on the other hand, your observed results do not match up with your expected outcomes, you need to spend time understanding why before moving forward.

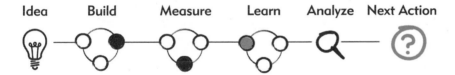

This might be accomplished in a number of ways:

I. Review Captured Artifacts

Revisit captured artifacts such as notes and recorded customer interviews in search of insights you might have missed before.

II. Conduct a Five Whys Analysis

Run a Five Whys session with other team members in search of deeper causes for your unexpected outcomes.

III. Do More Extensive Data Mining

Analyze your data differently or dig into a different data set of micro metrics that might help you uncover patterns of causality in your observed results.

IV. Run a Follow-up Learning Experiment

As metrics can tell you only what occurred—not why—sometimes the best course of action is to run a follow-up learning experiment designed to gather more data.

2. ANALYZE YOUR STRATEGY

Next you analyze your observed results at the strategy level. Based on your observed results, a Validation Plan can go into one of four possible next states:

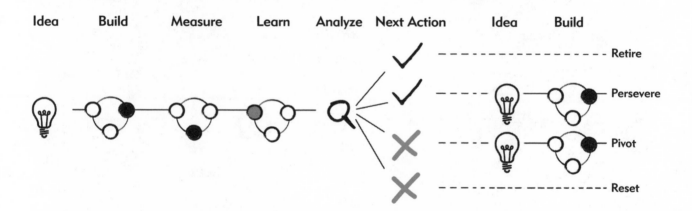

I. Retire

This is when you successfully break the constraint and achieve the macro goal that you set out to achieve with this strategy. You retire this strategy and move on to prioritizing the next promising ideas in your backlog.

II. Persevere

This is when you gather enough positive signals to warrant staying the course on the current strategy. You can move on to the next step of analyzing the strategy against your models, which helps you decide the next experiment to run.

For example, if your overall strategy was launching a new feature, your first experiment might involve testing interest in that feature. Getting enough positive signals, as dictated by your models, gives you permission to stay the course.

III. Pivot

This is when you don't gather enough positive signals to stay the course, but you know why, and aren't ready yet to give up on the strategy. A pivot represents a change in direction based on newly uncovered learning while staying focused on the goal.

For example, if your overall strategy was testing for Problem/Solution Fit, your first experiment might involve finding interview leads using your blog. If you fail to get enough leads but know the reason is that your blog audience does not overlap with your ideal early customer segment, you would not give up on the overall strategy but pivot to testing a different channel, such as guest blogging or advertising.

IV. Reset

This is when you gather enough negative signals to invalidate a strategy. As there is clearly no point in staying the course, you make a decision to reallocate resources to more promising ideas in your backlog.

3. UPDATE YOUR MODELS

Finally, you need to ensure that you always keep your models updated after each experiment—especially your customer factory model, which will change a lot more frequently than your Lean Canvas and traction models. That said, remember that finding a business model that works is a search-versus-execution problem. Much as you pit several competing strategies or experiments against one another, you also pit several competing business models against one another. For this reason, it's just as important to frequently visit your business model stories and ensure that they reflect your latest learning.

4. DECIDE NEXT ACTIONS

With your analysis done, you are now ready to decide next actions. Based on your results and updated models, you reevaluate whether the current constraint is broken and, if so, you search for a new constraint. Remember that the steps in your customer factory are highly interdependent on one another. Changes in one area often have ripple effects in other areas. When you don't constantly monitor the entire system at a macro level, inertia can set in and lead you to fall into the local optimization trap. This is when you fail to recognize that your current efforts have successfully broken a constraint and you keep on optimizing further—at the expense of tackling the next weakest link.

From this analysis, you then decide to double down on certain strategies, discontinue others, and maybe even add new ones.

Lean Canvas Case Study

A great way to internalize the GO LEAN framework is to see it in action. I'm going to walk you through a case study on how we applied this framework to an onboarding problem we encountered with the online Lean Canvas tool.

BACKGROUND

I was first exposed to Alex Osterwalder's Business Model Canvas (BMC) in May 2009. I was immediately drawn to the idea of capturing a business model on a single page. But after modeling a number of my own products, I felt the BMC's strategic perspective on business modeling might be better suited to more established products and a

Having no problems in your business model is a problem.

better fit for consultants than entrepreneurs. Coming from a customer-centric and lean background, I found it missing two critical boxes: Problem and Solution.

As the BMC was released under a Creative Commons license and welcomed remixing, I published my adaptation, Lean Canvas, in a blog post in August 2009. This post quickly rose to become one of my top blog posts of all time.* By September 2009, I launched an online tool with the help of another entrepreneur, Lukas Fittl.

GOAL

Even though the Lean Canvas was originally designed with high-tech lean startups in mind, its usage spread quickly across a much wider customer segment including other startups, large companies, and universities. We revised our goal from reaching 10,000 users to reaching 100,000 users. By January 2012, we had crossed that goal and were signing up hundreds of new users per week. But with expansion comes challenge.

OBSERVE AND ORIENT

While we were signing up more people than before, our activation rate started dropping. We define user activation as the completion of six out of the nine blocks in the Lean Canvas. Our activation rates were close to 70 percent when we first launched. They were now hovering at 35 percent. This became the key constraint to break.

---

* You can read more about the changes I made to the Business Model Canvas and why here: http://leanstack.com/why-lean-canvas/.

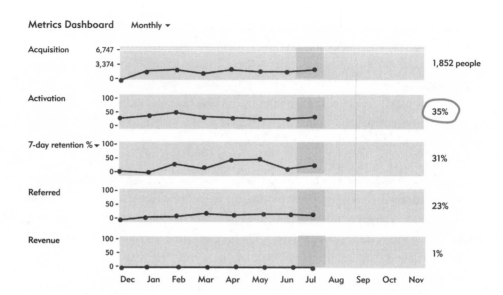

We started by mapping out our activation subfunnel (micro metrics) to understand where users were dropping off.

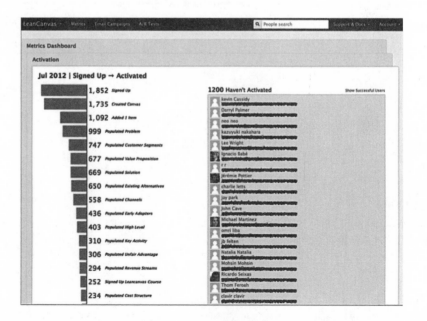

Lean Canvas activation subfunnel showing the list of steps users took toward creating their first business model.

Once we mapped out this funnel, ideas immediately started flowing. It was interesting to observe the diversity of possible solutions my team generated to the same problem:

1. Because this was a long, multistep funnel, my designer wanted to improve usability by reducing steps and optimizing this flow.
2. My developer wanted to build a better onboarding flow that would interactively walk users through the process of creating a canvas.
3. The marketer in me just wanted to keep adding more users through my blog, book, and workshop channels.

We even got around to implementing a number of these ideas, but none of them made a significant enough dent in the activation rate.

LEARN, LEVERAGE, LIFT

The reason all our experiments were falling flat was that each of us had guessed the cause for the low activation rates but none of our experiments were agreeing with our guesses.

EXPERIMENT

All our previous experiments had been prematurely geared toward lifting the constraint (by jumping to a solution), which is an expensive route, especially when you are guessing. We realized that we needed to first learn more about the constraint. So we devised a two-week learning experiment.

> Knowing where the problems exist is not enough. You have to get to why.

The idea was simple. We would simply ask people why they weren't completing their canvases after a set time delay. From our data, we learned that 80 percent of our users completed their canvases within the first seven days of signing up. So we built a feature that automatically sent out a short e-mail after a week to those users who had started creating a canvas but never finished. Not everyone responded, but

| You don't need lots of users to learn.

we got enough responses after two weeks to formulate a new set of hypotheses.

ANALYZE

These were the top three reasons our users cited for not completing their canvases:

1. Too busy
2. Needed more information
3. Just checking out the tool

We ran an internal Five Whys on each of them and followed up with several users via e-mail and phone calls for further clarification. We quickly validated that people weren't getting stuck because the canvas was confusing to fill out, but because they didn't know what to put in the boxes. This line of thinking was further corroborated by the fact that these users were also new to the Lean Startup methodology. Giving them a blank canvas to fill out was akin to giving someone a word processor and asking them to write a short story.

NEXT ACTION

A live customer conversation is often the best way to uncover what you don't know that you don't know.

With this new data, our next action was formulating a set of possible solutions. We decided the most promising strategy was launching a short video course to teach new users how to create a Lean Canvas. This started our next two-week cycle.

LEARN, LEVERAGE, LIFT

I already taught a half-day workshop about how to fill out the Lean Canvas, which was an asset we could leverage. But because users also reported being busy, we decided to break the course into smaller bite-size lessons delivered over seven days.

We set this experiment up as a parallel split test where only half of new users would see the video course. That way, we were isolating and measuring the impact of the video course.

Can you guess what the results were?

Experiments

7-Day Course A/B test (A/B Test)
Test activation after 7-day course

Option A:	`false`	**4,745 participants**	**1,500 converted**	**31.6% (5% better showing than option B)**
Option B:	`true`	**4,727 participants**	**1,419 converted**	**30.0%** <u>show</u>

There are 9,472 participants in this experiment. The best choice is option A: it converted at 31.6% (5% better than option B). With 95% probability this result is statistically significant. Option C converted at 30.0%. Option A selected as the best alternative.

We measured no significant impact in activation rates between the cohorts. In fact, if you look closely, there was even a slight dip in the activation rate of those users who watched the video. (Option B)

ANALYZE

While this seemed like a promising approach at the start, the results did not support our initial enthusiasm. The right next action would have been to declare this a failed strategy and look for an alternative solution. But we didn't. Here's why.

Even though we did not measure an activation rate increase, we got an overwhelming number of positive comments below the videos and several e-mails thanking us for making the video. This indicated that the videos weren't a complete waste and were having some benefit beyond increasing the activation rate.

It's okay to focus on a single key metric, but you ALWAYS have to monitor the entire customer factory.

Our split testing tool (like most off-the-shelf tools) was designed to measure only a single metric in a split test. We built a new dashboard to analyze the data differently and discovered that people who watched the videos were indeed creating their canvases faster. The average completion time of canvases dropped from seven days to three days. Retention was also higher for users exposed to the video. Over time, this cohort of users also resulted in a higher conversion to paid users.

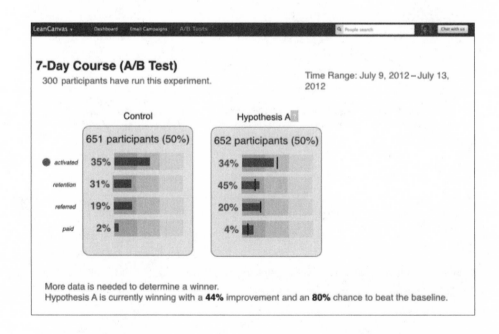

We didn't end up killing the video course strategy but doubled down on it. Fast-forwarding to today, we have invested heavily in e-mail and content marketing and built several multiweek free and paid courses that guide users through their journey as entrepreneurs. Each of these campaigns has been attributed to steady lifts in both retention and revenue.

This case study again drives home the point that blindly focusing on any one local metric is not effective.

Key Takeaways

Increasing throughput is the only macro that matters.

- Instead of running away from failure, dig in your heels and ask why.
- Breakthrough insights are usually hidden within failed experiments.
- Replace the word "failure" with "unexpected outcomes."

CHAPTER 10

Avoid the Curse of Specialization

WE'RE HIGHLY PRONE TO SUBCONSCIOUS BIASES WHEN DEVISING solutions to problems we're eager to solve. While the GO LEAN framework helps you expose the "right" problems or constraints to tackle, your strategies are still vulnerable to the innovator's bias. In my Lean Canvas case study from the last chapter, for instance, given our problem of a low user activation rate:

- My developers wanted to build more features,
- My designers wanted to improve usability, and
- My marketers wanted to optimize landing pages and run ads.

"To raise new questions, new possibilities, to regard old problems from a new angle, requires creative imagination."

—ALBERT EINSTEIN

Different team members will see different solutions to the same problem based on their specialized training. This is the innovator bias at work, which by itself is not a problem. It is a problem only if you limit the diversity of ideas. In order to achieve breakthrough, you have to continually tap into a large source of new ideas.

The real answer to the question "Where do good ideas come from?" is that good ideas can come from anywhere.

The challenge, of course, is that good ideas are rare and often indistinguishable from bad ideas at the beginning. So you need a robust process that on the one hand allows you to source a large diversity of ideas, and on the other hand lets you quickly distinguish good ideas from bad ideas. This chapter will show you how to do this using LEAN sprints.

What Is a LEAN Sprint?

A LEAN sprint is a time-boxed iteration cycle for sourcing, ranking, and testing new ideas for moving your business model forward, that is, for breaking constraints and increasing customer throughput. Simply put, LEAN sprints help you implement the GO LEAN framework across your team.

The right time box for a LEAN sprint is determined by the stage of your product and the size of your team. I recommend starting with two-week sprints and adjusting from there. Here's what a typical two-week sprint looks like:

The sprint start and end are marked by two meeting ceremonies: the **sprint planning meeting** and the **sprint review meeting**. This is where the team comes together to plan strategy and experiment-level activities and share results. During the sprint, the team also meets regularly to coordinate task-level activities using a short daily **stand-up meeting**.

One of the things you might have immediately picked up on was the number of meetings during sprints. I know the last thing you want is more meetings. However, meetings run *well* create time-boxed opportunities for focused conversation—which is key to success.

> The true job of an entrepreneur is systematically derisking her business model through a series of conversations.

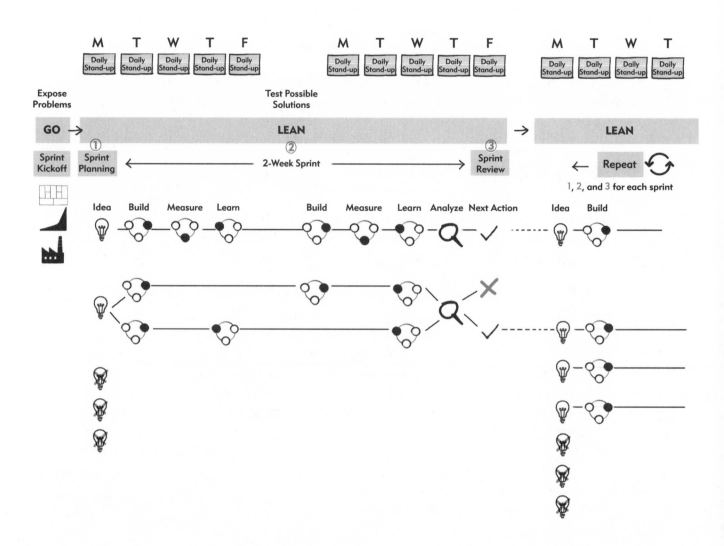

Most meetings don't work because:

1. There isn't a set agenda.

   While the reason for a meeting might be known in advance, most meetings just go with the flow, which sometimes, but not always, leads to actual progress being made. Like the interview scripts in *Running Lean*, LEAN sprint meetings are driven by a metascript designed to accomplish certain key learning objectives.

2. There isn't enough active participation.

   There are usually just one or two people doing most of the talking, while everyone else listens. LEAN sprint meetings are hands-on and require everyone's participation.

3. There's isn't enough original thinking.

   When HiPPOs and peers bias meetings, they can quickly devolve into groupthink. LEAN sprint meetings use an align-diverge-converge design thinking technique, developed at IDEO (a design and consulting firm), for fighting groupthink and enabling original thinking.

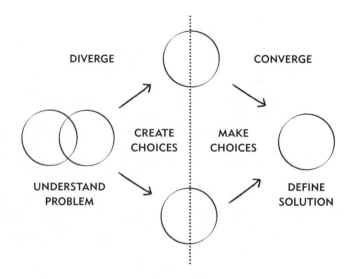

DIVERGE   CONVERGE

CREATE
CHOICES

MAKE
CHOICES

UNDERSTAND
PROBLEM

DEFINE
SOLUTION

In this technique, meetings are used only for alignment and decisions—not free-form discussion or group brainstorming.

HOW IS THE LEAN SPRINT DIFFERENT FROM AN AGILE ITERATION OR A SCRUM SPRINT?

If you come from a software background, you have most likely been exposed to the scrum/agile methodology, and would have noticed several similarities between a scrum sprint and the LEAN sprint. LEAN sprints are heavily influenced by agile and scrum practices, like the meeting ceremonies, but there are some key differences.

1. The goals are different.

   While the goal of a scrum sprint is demonstrating "build velocity," the goal of a LEAN sprint is demonstrating "traction velocity." It is not enough to build a great product or feature during an iteration, or just to demonstrate learning. You have to build, measure, learn, *and* demonstrate how your product or feature affects one or more of the key levers for traction.

2. The participants are different.

    Scrum and agile are typically developer-only practices. LEAN sprints, on the other hand, require the complete team, including your internal and external stakeholders.

3. Time boxing does not dictate build or release cadence.

    I am still an advocate for using kanban (or just-in-time) techniques for continuous delivery. Time boxes in a LEAN sprint are used only to force a decision and do not drive the release cycle. You can still choose to practice continuous delivery or a more traditional schedule-based release cycle as you see fit.

HOW IS THE LEAN SPRINT DIFFERENT FROM A DESIGN SPRINT?

If you come from a design background, you have most likely been exposed to the design sprint created and popularized by Google Ventures.

Design sprints also draw from the agile framework but incorporate design thinking techniques to help teams solve design problems in five days. Cross-functional team members are recruited from across the organization and then spend five intense days working on the design problem through lots of brainstorming, rapid prototyping, and user testing. At the end of the sprint, winning solutions are decided and handed off to implementation teams. The sprint team is then disassembled.

While LEAN sprints also draw inspiration from several design thinking (and design sprint) techniques, they are intended for more general problem/solution exploration. The activity cadence is also less intense on the teams. Unlike with design sprints, the goal isn't assembling a short-term SWAT-style team that comes together to solve a big problem one time. Rather the goal is assembling a long-term product team that continually solves big problems from one sprint to the next.

The Five Stages of a LEAN Sprint

There are five stages to running a LEAN sprint. These stages use overlapping align-diverge-converge cycles to provide the right balance between individual thinking and group collaboration:

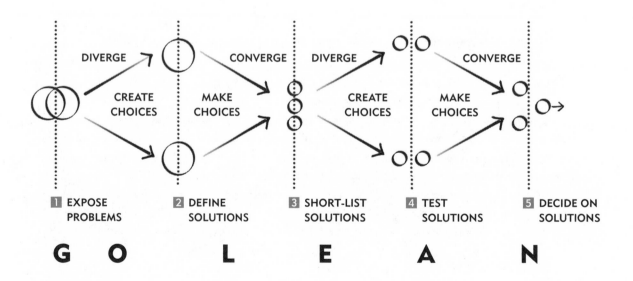

1 EXPOSE PROBLEMS   2 DEFINE SOLUTIONS   3 SHORT-LIST SOLUTIONS   4 TEST SOLUTIONS   5 DECIDE ON SOLUTIONS

G   O   L   E   A   N

1. **Expose Problems:** What is the constraint?

   The team comes together in a presprint meeting to align around a common understanding of the business model constraints.

2. **Define Solutions:** How might we break this constraint?

   The team then diverges to individually generate solutions captured on one or more Validation Plans.

3. **Short-list Solutions:** Select the best strategies.

   These solutions are then shared, ranked, and short-listed in a sprint planning meeting that officially kicks off the sprint.

4. **Test Solutions:** Test the strategies with experiments.

   The team diverges again to test these solutions.

5. **Decide on Solutions:** Decide next actions.

   Results are analyzed and next actions decided in a sprint review meeting. The cycle then repeats.

The rest of this chapter will walk through the details of running through these five stages.

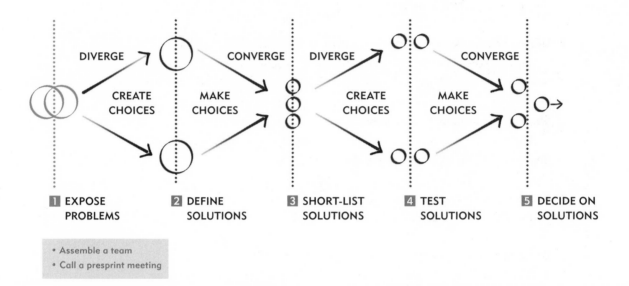

1. EXPOSE PROBLEMS

The first stage is aligning the team around the "right" problems or constraints. It is important to involve every role in the company to avoid the "curse of specialization." So start with assembling the right team.

Assemble the Right Team

You need to start by rethinking your team structure. I am not going to weigh in on the merits of remote versus distributed teams or open versus closed workspaces. A LEAN sprint team needs to maximize for speed, learning, and focus:

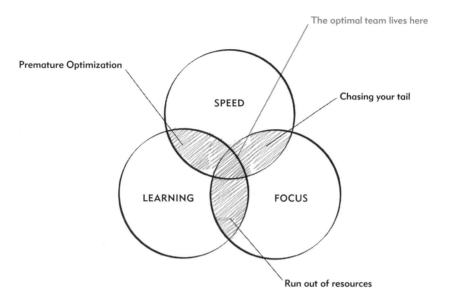

To do this, teams need to be small, multidisciplinary, and semiautonomous.

Small

Metcalfe's law, that "the value of a communication system grows at approximately the square of the number of users of the system," has a corollary when it comes to project teams:

> "The efficiency of a team is approximately the inverse of the square of the number of members in the team."
>
> —MARC HEDLUND

As a team grows in size, communication breaks down and devolves into group-think. A good rule of thumb on team size is instituting a two-pizza team rule:

> "The two pizza team rule: Any team should be small
> enough that it could be fed with two pizzas."
>
> —JEFF BEZOS, AMAZON

Instead of creating one large extended team per product, consider splitting into many small teams.

Multidisciplinary

Next, these teams need to be complete teams. If you have to rely on shared external resources to get work done, your throughput will be affected. Like your customer factory, the output of your organization is also driven by a system of interconnected processes. When deliverables are created in silos and driven by potentially different sets of internal KPIs (key performance indicators), you run into the same issues of compromising your overall throughput at the expense of these local metrics.

More important, you need a cross-functional team to be able to source a diversity of ideas, which is critical for overcoming the curse of specialization.

In *Running Lean*, I described a complete team as having build, design, and marketing expertise. In order to run effective sprints, you will additionally need someone to take on the lead role of sprint master. This person will be responsible for taking the team through all the stages.

Lean Sprint Team Roles:

LEAN Sprint Master

Core Team:
Designers
Developers
Marketers

Stakeholders:

Advisers

Investors

Subject-Matter Experts

Directors or Executives

Semiautonomous

On the one hand, your team needs to be empowered to do whatever is needed to achieve the goal. If they have to constantly get permission to test ideas, that will affect their speed of implementation.

But the other extreme—granting a team full autonomy, where they answer to no one—is also dangerous. This is the traditional skunk works or R&D model where the team is given a large budget and charged to "innovate." One thing is certain—all the money will get spent. The team will often move off-site into more creative spaces to give themselves room to think differently from the legacy business. While it's sound in principle, when this kind of autonomy is left unchecked, individual passion (or bias) also finds a way to rear its ugly head.

THE DEEP SPACE INTRAPRENEURSHIP ANALOGY

Think of intrapreneurship as launching an exploratory probe into space.

If you shoot out too far, you will get lost, eventually run out of resources, and die a quiet death.

Even if you do manage to return, you will probably bring back something so alien to the core business that you will be killed off by some vice president.

The key to success is not aiming for deep space, but aiming to orbit a specific target (albeit fuzzy) *and* maintaining regular communication with an executive sponsor on the home planet.

The target establishes a goal worth pursuing. Regular communication and external accountability manage expectations and safeguard your return.

Adapted from a conversation with Manish Mehta, who was an early intrapreneur at Dell.

The right balance is establishing an external accountability system that provides the team with autonomy to explore solutions while staying grounded to certain core business model constraints and goals.

Involvement of your internal and external stakeholders during LEAN sprints is key. If you are in a startup, these stakeholders can be external advisers and/or investors. In a corporate environment, they can be subject-matter experts and executive project sponsors. Even if you are a bootstrapped entrepreneur, I highly recommend creating some sort of an ad hoc advisory board for this purpose.

Run a Presprint Meeting

If this is your first sprint, it is best to call a presprint meeting to set expectations, share the goal of the sprint, and orient the team. In future sprints, the learning momentum from each sprint automatically carries over to the next sprint. So additional kickoffs are generally not required.

Attendees
Required: Core team
Optional: Stakeholders

Duration
45 minutes

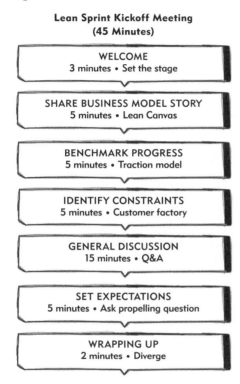

**Lean Sprint Kickoff Meeting
(45 Minutes)**

WELCOME
3 minutes • Set the stage

SHARE BUSINESS MODEL STORY
5 minutes • Lean Canvas

BENCHMARK PROGRESS
5 minutes • Traction model

IDENTIFY CONSTRAINTS
5 minutes • Customer factory

GENERAL DISCUSSION
15 minutes • Q&A

SET EXPECTATIONS
5 minutes • Ask propelling question

WRAPPING UP
2 minutes • Diverge

Welcome (Set the Stage)

(3 minutes)

Briefly set the stage by reinforcing your motivation for running LEAN sprints. Then walk through the agenda items.

Share Business Model Story (Lean Canvas)

(5 minutes)

Spend five minutes on your business model story using the latest snapshot of your Lean Canvas(es). Here's a suggested order for walking through the canvas:

PROBLEM	SOLUTION	UNIQUE VALUE PROPOSITION	UNFAIR ADVANTAGE	CUSTOMER SEGMENTS
List your customers' top 3 problems	Outline possible solution for each problem	Single, clear, compelling message that turns an unaware visitor into an interested prospect	Something that can't be easily copied or bought	List your target customers and users
2	**4**	**3**	**9**	**1**
EXISTING ALTERNATIVES	**KEY METRICS**	**HIGH-LEVEL CONCEPT**	**CHANNELS**	**EARLY ADOPTERS**
List how these problems are solved today	List key numbers telling how your business is doing today **8**	List your X for Y analogy (e.g., YouTube = Flickr for videos)	List your path to customers	List characteristics of your ideal customer

COST STRUCTURE	REVENUE STREAMS
List your fixed and variable costs	List your sources of revenue
7	**6**

Lean Canvas is adapted from The Business Model Canvas (www.businessmodelgeneration.com) and is licensed under the Creative Commons Attribution-Share Alike 3.0 Un-ported License.

The goal shouldn't be to simply read the canvas aloud, because people can read faster than you can talk. Instead, use your canvas as a visual aid. While your team scans the canvas, focus instead on the backstory behind the business:

- How did you stumble on this customer or problem?
- How long has the project been running?
- What's been done so far?

Benchmark Progress (Traction Model)

(5 minutes)

Next, focus on your traction model. Starting with your minimum success criteria, describe your desired traction model. Plot your current customer throughput rate against it and identify the stage of your product: Problem/Solution Fit, Product/Market Fit, or Scale.

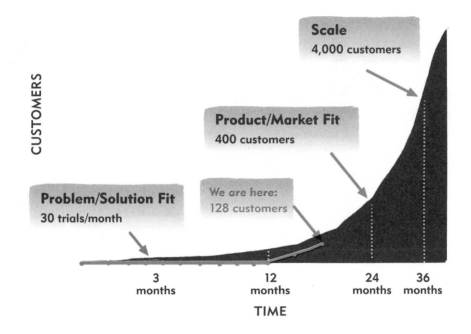

Identify Constraints (Customer Factory)

(5 minutes)

Finally, use your customer factory dashboard to identify the constraint in the business model. The goal isn't getting to root causes but simply highlighting hot spots.

These chalk circles frame the problem areas and focus the team.

Week 90: Testing Different Pricing Models

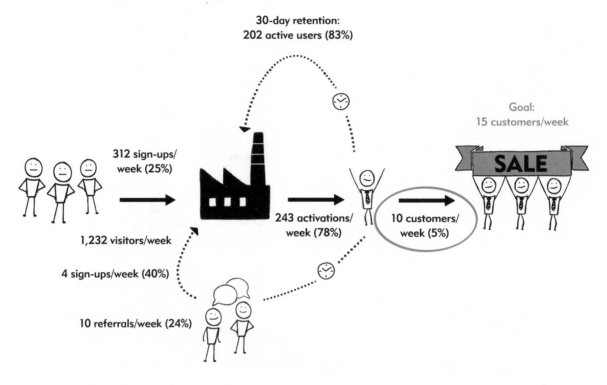

General Discussion (Q&A)

(15 minutes)

Pause here and allow your team to ask any clarifying questions. However, avoid any conversations that start veering into designing solutions. Remind them that capturing their solutions is the purpose of the next stage.

"To achieve great things, two things are needed: a plan and not quite enough time."

—LEONARD BERNSTEIN

Set Expectations (Ask Propelling Question)

(5 minutes)

The next step is charging your team with big goals under tight constraints. Remember that constraints are healthy and even required for forcing actions and driving innovation. Limiting your team size is such a constraint. Another is limiting your sprint time box. While it can be scary to have a deadline, deadlines are essential.

Decide on a sprint cadence you think you can maintain sustainably. If unsure, start with two-week cycles and adjust from there.

Wrapping Up

(2 minutes)

Wrap up the meeting by stating your propelling question. For example: "How can we improve paid conversion rates without building more features?" Then get everyone to work.

2. DEFINE SOLUTIONS

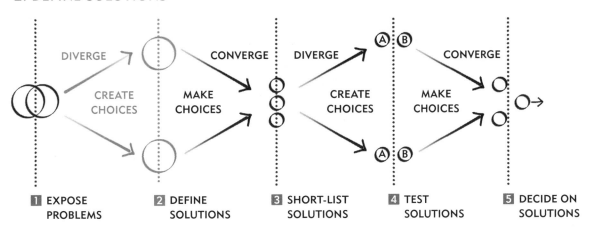

The team then goes off to formulate plans for breaking the constraint and achieving the goal. Further analysis is usually needed to do this, which each team member does individually. This avoids groupthink and allows for a wider diversity of ideas. The team applies the three focusing steps—Learn, Leverage, Lift—to capture their proposals on one or more Validation Plans.

3. SHORT-LIST SOLUTIONS

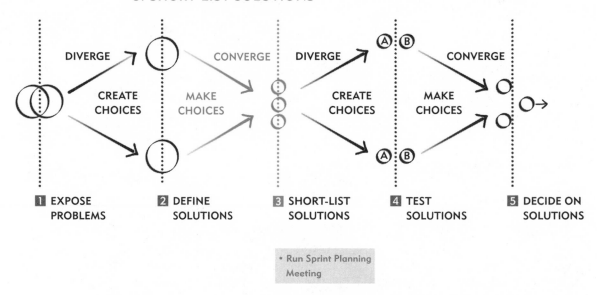

If your team did a good job sourcing ideas, chances are high that you'll end up with more proposals than you have time to test during a sprint. You will need to rank and short-list these proposals—which should be done in the sprint planning meeting.

The Sprint Planning Meeting

Purpose
The sprint planning meeting officially starts the sprint. The purpose of this meeting is to review, rank, and short-list Validation Plans and define experiments for the current sprint.

Attendees

Required: Core team

Recommended: Stakeholders

Duration

Usually an hour per week of iteration—for example, a two-week sprint kicks off with a two-hour planning meeting

Agenda

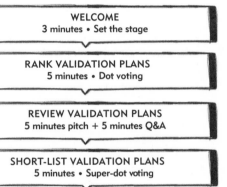

**Lean Sprint Kickoff Meeting
(120 Minutes)**

WELCOME
3 minutes • Set the stage

RANK VALIDATION PLANS
5 minutes • Dot voting

REVIEW VALIDATION PLANS
5 minutes pitch + 5 minutes Q&A

SHORT-LIST VALIDATION PLANS
5 minutes • Super-dot voting

REVIEW EXPERIMENTS
5 minutes pitch + 5 minutes Q&A per experiment

SET EXPECTATIONS
5 minutes per experiment

WRAPPING UP
2 minutes • Get to work

Welcome (Set the Stage)

(3 minutes)

Share the agenda with the team and set the stage.

Rank Validation Plans (Dot Voting)

(5 minutes)

How many Validation Plans should you approve? Until you establish your team's sprint velocity (or capacity), a good rule of thumb is to divide your team's size by two to determine the target number of proposals you can test in a sprint. So for a team of five, the maximum number of Validation Plans to aim for is three. If you feel you have more capacity after sizing the selected proposals, feel free to adjust upward.

Constraining your work-in-progress (WIP) limit this way is another common practice taken from Lean Thinking to maximize a team's throughput and reduce the amount of work "nearly done." Lean production principles consider excess WIP to be a form of waste because unfinished work ties up resources that could be generating higher returns elsewhere.

With the WIP established, the team gets to work ranking the Validation Plans. The goal should be striving for a meritocratic approach that surfaces the best proposals without bias or peer influence. I recommend leaving the Validation Plans anonymous at first and using a dot voting method for ranking them.

Dot Voting

These One-Page Validation Plans are made public to the team by either pasting them up on a wall, handing out copies, or projecting them on a screen. Each team member is given a sheet of dot stickers (or some fixed number of votes) which they place on their favorite proposals. They can place more than one vote on each Validation Plan to show a strong preference. After the voting, the proposals are ranked from high to low and the top (WIP × 2) number of proposals are selected for further review. So in the example above where the WIP was three, select the top six Validation Plans for review.

The logic behind this silent voting is that the best ideas usually stand out on their own. This process works far better than letting people explain their ideas first—which, as you can imagine, burns a lot of time.

RANKING CRITERIA TO CONSIDER

While everyone will use their own internal ranking criteria, I suggest sharing the following guidelines for ranking ideas across two axes:

- the potential upside of the Validation Plan, and
- the depth of the analysis.

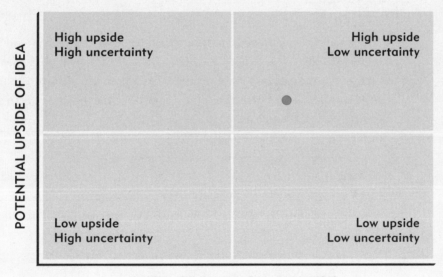

While there is a place and time for relying on hunches, priority should be given to those proposals that back the hunch with empirical reasoning. This may be the result of data analysis, qualitative learning, or even citing a close analog worth imitating.

What about technical feasibility or implementation effort? With practice, every big strategy can be broken into a small, fast, additive experiment. So the initial emphasis shouldn't be on implementation effort, but rather on testing whether the strategy is worth pursuing at all.

The originator of the Validation Plan should also be prepared to describe a first experiment. If this Validation Plan gets selected, there will be more time later in the meeting to further refine the experiment.

Review Validation Plans (Pitch + Q&A)

(5 minutes per pitch and per experiment)

The Validation Plan originators are then revealed and each originator spends five minutes sharing his Validation Plan with the team. As with the Lean Canvas walkthrough, the goal isn't simply reading the proposal aloud, but using it as a visual aid. At this point, it's perfectly okay to supplement the Validation Plan with other supporting artifacts such as:

- Customer interview results or other qualitative research
- Wireframes and mock-ups
- Screenshots and short demos of other analog solutions
- A scoped-down Lean Canvas that homes in on a specific customer subsegment

It is implied that anyone submitting a Validation Plan should come to the meeting ready to present this supporting evidence. After the overview, another five minutes are set aside for questions.

Short-list Validation Plans (Super-Dot Voting)

(5 minutes)

After the reviews, the proposals are ranked once more using super votes. These are simply a different colored sticker. Everyone is given one or two of these "special" stickers and they are used to rank the very best ideas.

Between the original dot voting and these super votes, it should be easy to short-list the final proposals to meet your WIP limit. While the goal is to strive for a meritocracy, that may be difficult to achieve given your company culture—which is okay to admit. Super votes allow for weighted voting to accommodate this. Simply give deciders, typically stakeholders, extra votes.

Review Experiments

(5 minutes per pitch and per experiment)

With your Validation Plans short-listed, the next step is reviewing experiments. Each Validation Plan originator then takes up to five minutes to outline:

- How will they test the strategy (experiment details)?
- How long will it take (time box)?
- What resources will they require (team, etc.)?

Another five minutes are set aside to review the experiment approach and possibly come up with a faster way to test the strategy.

Set Expectations

(5 minutes per experiment)

Once the experiment approach is defined, the team then plays the expected outcomes estimation game. In three minutes (set a timer), each team member individually writes down her expected outcomes on a piece of paper. You can choose to share all the estimates with everyone or just share the spread across the estimates. The goal of the estimation game is improving judgment. The true value of the exercise will be realized during the sprint review meeting. For now, just record the votes and move on.

Wrapping Up

(2 minutes)

Before you leave, ensure that everyone has clarity on the tasks ahead.

4. TEST SOLUTIONS

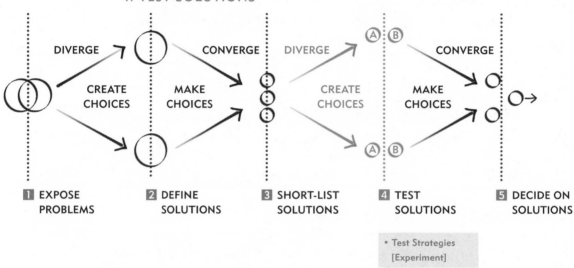

Experiments then go through the build-measure-learn cycle. It is okay to run more than one experiment per Validation Plan during a sprint, but all experiments need to complete within the sprint time-box window. During the sprint, the core team typically holds short daily **stand-up meetings** for coordinating lower-level tasks among team members.

The Daily Stand-up Meeting

Instituting a daily stand-up or daily huddle is a best practice for ensuring that work is progressing as planned. This is not a status meeting but rather a quick check-in.

Required: Core team

Recommended: Stakeholders

When

Once per day, typically in the morning

Duration

No more than 15 minutes

Agenda

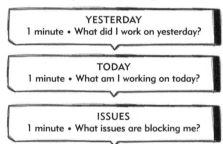

**Lean Sprint Stand-up Meeting
(15 Minutes max)**

YESTERDAY
1 minute • What did I work on yesterday?

TODAY
1 minute • What am I working on today?

ISSUES
1 minute • What issues are blocking me?

You quickly go around the room and have every team member spend no more than three minutes outlining:

1. What did I work on yesterday?
2. What am I working on today?
3. What issues are blocking me?

The goal is not to problem solve but rather to collect the updates and allow team members to coordinate as needed outside the stand-up.

Analyze Results

As experiments complete, results are **Analyzed** against the goal. Often more learning experiments or analysis is required prior to the sprint review meeting, so make sure you leave yourselves enough time.

5. DECIDE ON SOLUTIONS

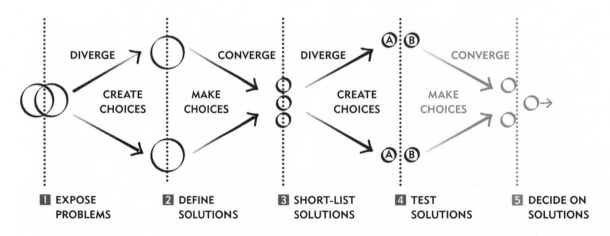

1 EXPOSE PROBLEMS   2 DEFINE SOLUTIONS   3 SHORT-LIST SOLUTIONS   4 TEST SOLUTIONS   5 DECIDE ON SOLUTIONS

• Run Sprint Review Meeting

At the end of the sprint, a **sprint review meeting** is held, where experiment results are presented and the appropriate **Next Actions** decided.

The Sprint Review Meeting

Purpose
The sprint review meeting officially ends the sprint. The purpose of this meeting is to review experiment results and decide on appropriate next actions across all the Validation Plans tested during the sprint.

Attendees
Required: Core team
Recommended: Stakeholders

Duration
60 minutes

Agenda

**Lean Sprint Review Meeting
(60 Minutes max)**

WELCOME
2 minutes • Set the stage

SHARE MACRO RESULTS
5 minutes • Customer factory

PRESENT EXPERIMENT RESULTS
5 minutes per experiment

DECIDE NEXT ACTIONS
10 minutes per experiment • Review analysis

WRAPPING UP
3 minutes • Identify next constraint

Welcome (Set the Stage)

(2 minutes)

Share the agenda with the team to set the stage.

Share Macro Results (Customer Factory)

(5 minutes)

Start by reviewing your updated customer factory dashboard with the team to determine whether the original constraint is broken. If so, celebrate your success and refocus the team toward the new constraint for the next sprint.

Present Experiment Results

(5 minutes per experiment)

Next, review all the experiments' results. Each Validation Plan originator spends five minutes sharing his results and analysis of his experiment(s) with the team. After the update, another five minutes are set aside for questions. This is the right time to award a prize to the winner of the estimation game, too.

Decide Next Actions (Review Analysis)

(10 minutes per experiment)

Based on the results of the experiment, the team then votes on one of four possible next actions to take with the Validation Plan:

    i. Retire (Move on to a new idea)
   ii. Persevere (Stay the course)
  iii. Pivot (Change direction)
   iv. Reset (Kill the idea)

Wrapping Up (Identify Next Constraint)

(3 minutes)

End the meeting by highlighting the next constraint and propelling question (which may remain unchanged). Ensure that your business model, traction model, and customer factory dashboards are all updated before you leave.

Key Takeaways

- Good ideas can come from anywhere.
- In order to achieve breakthrough, you need an effective process for sourcing, ranking, and testing ideas.
- LEAN sprints are a time-boxed process for doing just that.
- Two weeks is a good starting length for your sprints.
- LEAN sprints require the full team.
- A LEAN sprint has five steps:
  1. Expose problems
  2. Define solutions
  3. Short-list solutions
  4. Test solutions
  5. Decide on solutions

CHAPTER 11

Hold Yourself Accountable

THUS FAR, WE HAVE FOCUSED ON INTERNAL TEAM CONVERSATIONS. THE primary objective of these conversations is to generate a diverse array of ideas and to keep the innovator's bias in check when evaluating problems and solutions. There is one other type of conversation that is just as important. This is the conversation you have with your external stakeholders. The primary objective of these conversations is to manage their expectations while holding yourself accountable.

While external stakeholder participation is encouraged in the types of meetings we covered in the last chapter, most stakeholders can't sustain the shorter cadence of LEAN sprints—they tend to be busy people. They are also more focused on macro results. This chapter will outline another type of conversation better suited to this purpose: the Progress Report.

Help Them Help You

External stakeholders like your mentors, board members, and/or investors are great sources of idea generation. But they often are poorly utilized for two main reasons:

First, we tend to share only good news with external stakeholders and hide any bad news for as long as we can. In the Lean Startup world, we call this "success theater."

Second, we tend to want to follow all the advice we are given, especially when it's coming from someone whom we respect or who is paying the bills. Left unchecked, this does more to distract and derail you than to help. This is the adviser whiplash problem.

ADVISER WHIPLASH

Ask ten people for advice on your idea and you'll get ten different prescriptions. Which one do you follow?

I see this all the time at some of the world's top accelerators. The problem is further exacerbated when teams have access to lots of recently successful entrepreneurs.

Seasoned entrepreneurs like to pay it forward by volunteering their time. A commendable gesture, but one that often leaves startups more confused than they were before.

When faced with conflicting advice, should entrepreneurs listen to the mentor who makes the most money or the mentor who makes the most sense?

UNCERTAINTY + CONFLICTING ADVICE = CHAOS

Recent success does not necessarily correlate with good advice. You can be a great entrepreneur but not a great teacher.

Tiger Woods is a better player than his coach, but his coach is a better teacher.

In my view, the adviser's job is *not* giving solutions but rather asking the right questions by using the Socratic method.

It is not about providing prescriptions, but about giving an honest diagnosis of key risks.

It is the entrepreneur's job not to blindly follow all the advice she is given, but rather to prioritize the advice based on current risks, which she then tests through small, fast, additive experiments.

It is also the entrepreneur's job to then double down on the best advice (and the best advisers) and ignore the rest.

The way to correctly leverage your external stakeholders is also twofold.

First, objectively present the same information to your external stakeholders that you shared with your internal teams. When you present skewed or selective data to potential advisers, their advice will be much less helpful. Try not to seek validation.

Next, always remember that you are the ultimate domain expert of your own business. You don't get a gold star for following advice, but for achieving results.

> "Adviser Paradox: Hire advisers for advice but don't follow it, apply it."
>
> —BABAK NIVI

You should be able to solicit advice from your external stakeholders at any time, but a great time for doing this is during quarterly board meetings. However, if possible, establish a more regular monthly reporting cadence where you can deliver the Progress Report and solicit more frequent feedback.

The Progress Report

Unlike sprint meetings, which are focused on strategies and experiments, the Progress Report focuses on macro metrics and business model goals.

Attendees
Required: Internal and external stakeholders
Optional: Core team

Duration
60 minutes

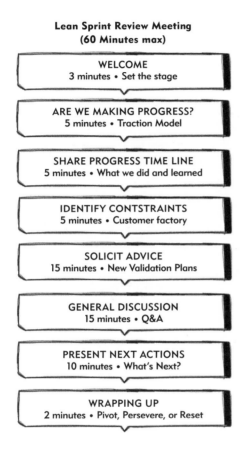

**Lean Sprint Review Meeting
(60 Minutes max)**

> **WELCOME**
> 3 minutes • Set the stage

> **ARE WE MAKING PROGRESS?**
> 5 minutes • Traction Model

> **SHARE PROGRESS TIME LINE**
> 5 minutes • What we did and learned

> **IDENTIFY CONTSTRAINTS**
> 5 minutes • Customer factory

> **SOLICIT ADVICE**
> 15 minutes • New Validation Plans

> **GENERAL DISCUSSION**
> 15 minutes • Q&A

> **PRESENT NEXT ACTIONS**
> 10 minutes • What's Next?

> **WRAPPING UP**
> 2 minutes • Pivot, Persevere, or Reset

Welcome (Set the Stage)

(3 minutes)

Set the stage for the meeting by quickly running through the agenda.

Are We Making Progress? (Traction Model)

(5 minutes)

Start by comparing your current throughput and customer throughput rates with the previous month's rates. Demonstrating traction (an increase in throughput) is the only macro metric that matters. The reason you want to show both throughput and customer throughput is to ensure that you are correctly attributing revenue to customers. If both these numbers are trending up and to the right, you are making progress. Otherwise, you have been spinning your wheels. It is also helpful to track your progress against your overall traction model and highlight any significant milestone crossings as you did during the sprint kickoff meeting. This sets the tone for the rest of the meeting.

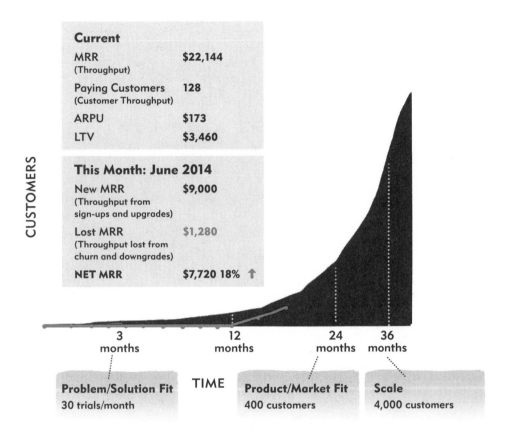

Share Progress Time Line (What We Did and Learned)

(5 minutes)

Next, present the activity time line from your LEAN sprints. Using a visualization like the one below, you can provide your external stakeholders with a bird's-eye view of all the activities your team has done since the last Progress Report meeting.

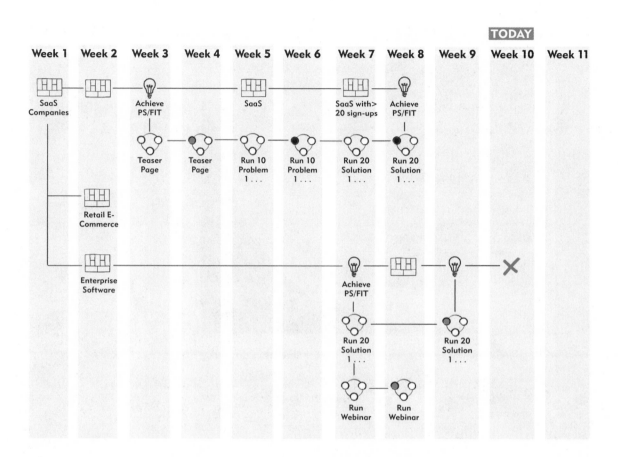

The visualization above shows the evolution of the USERcycle product and highlights.

- A few additional business model variants (Retail E-commerce and Enterprise Software) that we created in addition to our initial SaaS Companies business model.

- The Validation Plan and experiments we ran to test two of these models: SaaS Companies and Enterprise Software.
- We successfully achieved Problem/Solution Fit with the SaaS Companies business model but not with the Enterprise Software business model.

You don't need to cover every detail. Simply highlight the most significant event markers in the time line as I just did. Your stakeholders will inevitably have more questions beyond this quick overview. If you have been diligent about keeping good records with your Validation Plans and Experiment Reports, you should be able to zoom in to any level of detail as needed.

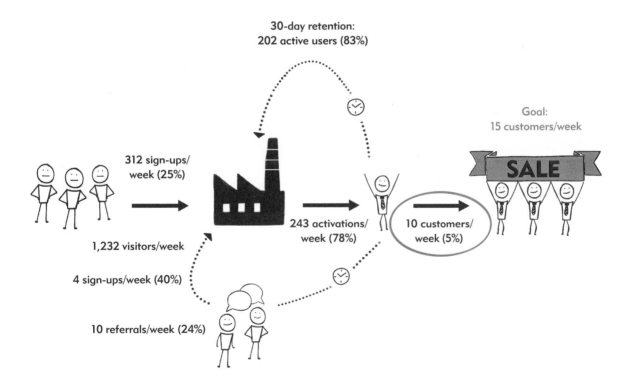

Identify Constraints (Customer Factory)

(5 minutes)

Then use your customer factory dashboard to identify the current constraint in the business model as you did in the sprint kickoff meeting.

Solicit Advice (New Validation Plans)

(15 minutes)

With your progress update and assessment of constraints out of the way, you can solicit potential solutions from your stakeholders.

Your stakeholders are just as vulnerable to groupthink as your core team. So instead of engaging in a general group discussion, it is best to solicit their feedback using a Note and Vote technique.

NOTE AND VOTE

The Note and Vote is a technique created by Google Ventures to help teams make group decisions quickly. Each person gets a pen and paper. In five minutes (set a timer), everyone writes down as many ideas as they can, without consulting anyone. Next, a timer is set for two minutes. Everyone picks one or two of their favorite items from the list.

Next, each member says his best idea aloud without any justification or elaboration. You capture all the ideas on a whiteboard.

Set a five-minute timer again, and this time, each person writes down one favorite idea from the whiteboard without any discussion. Once the timer goes off, everyone states their selections and you tally them up.

General Discussion (Q&A)

(15 minutes)

Pick the top three ideas and spend up to five minutes discussing each one. If more time is needed to flesh out details, follow up after the meeting. The goal at this stage isn't to define all the details but to create a backlog of potential strategies to test in your future sprints.

Present Next Actions (What's Next?)

(10 minutes)

Next, present your plans for the next month. Highlight the main strategies you will be testing and why.

Wrapping Up (Pivot, Persevere, or Reset)

(2 minutes)

End the meeting with a pivot, persevere, or reset vote.

Key Takeaways

- Use your models, strategies, and experiments to hold yourself accountable.
- Traction, or increasing customer throughput, is the only macro measure of progress.
- External accountability is key for making progress.
- Stakeholders are an often untapped idea generation source.
- Use Progress Reports to source new ideas and LEAN sprints to test the best candidates.

CONCLUSION

Are Entrepreneurs Born or Made?

I often get asked to weigh in on the age-old question of whether entrepreneurs are made or born.

> I believe that true entrepreneurs are born—not made.

Much like roller coasters, startups are inherently uncertain. One day you could be on top of the world, full of confidence, believing that your vision will change the world. But the next day, given the same exact conditions, you could be curled up in a ball—full of doubt both in yourself and in your vision.

I believe there's something intrinsic in entrepreneurs' DNA that lets them live—even thrive—under conditions of extreme uncertainty. I once heard an analogy that compared entrepreneurs to deep-sea fish. If you take fish at the surface down to the bottom of the ocean they will die. They can't survive the pressure and dark environment down there.

Deep-sea fish, on the other hand, have learned to survive under these harsh conditions. But interestingly, if you take the deep-sea fish up to the surface, they too will die. That's because they have not only learned to survive at the bottom of the ocean—they have come to need this constant pressure and challenging environment.

If my theory is right, then there is an upper limit to how many true entrepreneurs we can create. On the other hand, I believe we are nowhere near this upper limit yet.

Entrepreneurship to date has been concentrated in only a few global hot spots, and most people have been held back mainly due to a lack of enough resources to get started and a fear or taboo around failure.

But all that is about to change. In fact, I see it happening already. I believe more entrepreneurs will arise in the next ten years than during any other time in history. Thanks to new methodologies and thinking processes like the ones described in this book, these entrepreneurs will be even more distributed and more successful than their predecessors.

But what has an even greater potential for impact is drawing a distinction between entrepreneurs and entrepreneurial thinking. While a natural disposition is a benefit, it will get you only so far. The discipline of defining, measuring, and communicating progress must be internalized before you can perform at your best. While I believe entrepreneurs are born a certain way, entrepreneurial thinking can be taught—which makes it limitless.

Join the Conversation

A book is never finished—only published.

I continue to share my learning on my blog (http://leanstack.com/blog) and in my workshops and boot camps (http://leanstack.com/learn).

Drop me a line anytime.

E-mail: ash@leanstack.com

Twitter: @ashmaurya

Skype: ashmaurya

Thanks for reading, and here's to your success!

ACKNOWLEDGMENTS

I've got one more case study for you. As you can imagine, launching a book is no different from launching any other product. I wrote *Scaling Lean* using much the same process as I used for my last book—by applying every technique in the book to the launch of the book.

The Idea Spark

In the last five years, I've been fortunate to have been surrounded by thousands of entrepreneurs from all over the world. These entrepreneurs trusted me enough to openly share their unique startup challenges with me, which was key to uncovering the right problems worth solving for this book. *Scaling Lean* would not have been possible without their questions, comments, and, most important, unwavering commitment to stress testing the ideas presented in this book.

Solution Exploration

Next, I'd like to thank my extended Lean Stack team—my alliance of like-minded entrepreneurs who helped me turn these problems into a set of possible solutions. For every idea presented in this book, there were numerous variants that didn't make the cut. Thank you Lukas Fittl, Emiliano Villarreal, Steve Odom, Ernesto Tagwerker, Ry Walker, Tima Kunayev, Jonathan Drake, and Vanessa Roberts for dog fooding everything in this book.

The Goal

I self-published my first book as a side project with an initial goal of selling ten thousand copies in two years. After that book went on to sell many more copies than that and spawned a full-time business, I decided to accordingly 10X my goal for this book.

Very early on, I sat down with Eric Ries, author of the bestseller *The Lean Startup*, for advice. He graciously walked me through everything he learned from his book launch. His advice was instrumental in helping me define my own goal and launch strategy. I'd like to additionally thank Tim Ferriss, Jack Canfield, Seth Godin, Guy Kawasaki, Michael Hyatt, Tucker Max, Ryan Holiday, Noah Kagan, and Tim Grahl for helping demystify the traditional publishing landscape.

The Hook

Turning a set of rough ideas into a coherent book is a daunting undertaking. When you first start out, most people don't see what you see. I want to thank my editor, Niki Papadopoulos, and my super agent, Stephen Hanselman, for seeing and believing in the vision of the book. Thank you, Niki, for your patience through dozens of rewrites as I wildly iterated from one version to another to define this book's unique value proposition.

Continual Feedback Loop

The key to writing a good book is building a continual feedback with readers. I want to thank Sean Murphy, Ramon Suarez, Tristan Kromer, David Romero, David Bland, Giff Constable, KC Chhipwadia, Kevin Dewalt, and Ben Yoskovitz for reviewing early drafts throughout the writing process.

And a particular shout out goes to my wife and life partner, Sasha Maurya, who meticulously reviewed every chapter and saw me through all the book decisions—big and small. Thank you.

Product Packaging

I realized early on that the ideas in this book would best be communicated through a visual format. I want to thank Todd Clark for giving life to my words and rough sketches with his minimal yet bold style of illustration. Finally, thanks to Niki Papadopoulos, Leah Trouwborst, and everyone else behind the scenes at Portfolio who helped create such a beautiful book.

Product Marketing

Writing a book is only the first step. Without a scalable path to customers, even the best products die a silent death. I want to thank Tom Morkes and his incredible team at Insurgent Publishing and Tara Gilbride and Kelsey Odorczyk at Portfolio for turning our high-level launch strategy into a series of actionable tactics and experiments.

As of this writing, it is too early to tell if our strategies and tactics got us to the goal.

Visit the full case study to find out:

"Journey to 100K copies"—LeanStack.com/journey-100k

INDEX

Bernstein, Leonard, 244

Bezos, Jeff, 238

Biases. *See also* Cognitive biases
    innovator's, 21–22, 258

Big data business models, 35

Bloom Energy, 153

Boeing 747 airplane wingspan, 197–98

Booked revenue, 9, 26

Bootstrapping, 53, 240

Bothsides of the Table (blog), 81

Bottlenecks, 142–46, 159
    defects, 145–46, 151
    finding, 146–47, 149–50
        exercise, 158–59
    product case study, 142–45

Breaking constraints, 168, 169
    focusing steps, 172–76

Breakthrough, achieving. *See* Achieving
    breakthrough

Brin, Sergey, 57

Brodsky, Norm, *The Knack,* 53

Build-first strategy, 3–4, 9

Build/Measure/Learn cycle, 168–69

Build velocity, 9, 10

Burlingham, Bo, *The Knack,* 53

Business models. *See also specific business
    models*
    archetypes. *See* Business model
        archetypes
    back-of-the-envelope test. *See* Business
        model test
    conditions to meet for, 25–26

definition of, 23–24

execution versus search for, 46–47

exercises
    creating variants, 48
    describing your story, 45
    modeling traction and trajectory,
        85–90
    presprint meetings, 241–42
    theory of constraints, 14–15, 142–43

Business model archetypes, 30–38, 45
    direct, 31–33
    marketplaces, 36–38
    multisided, 33–36

Business Model Canvas (BMC), 24, 220–21.
    See also Lean Canvas

Business Model Innovation Factory, The
    (Kaplan), 23

Business model test, 49–72
    ballparking exercise, 71
    ballpark number, 52–53
    converting minimum success criteria to
        customer throughput, 58–64
    determining minimum success criteria,
        56–58
    inputs versus ouputs, 50–51
    key takeaways, 72
    testing/refining business model
        against minimum success criteria,
        64–68
    USERcycle case study, 53–68

Business plans, 3–4

Buyers, in marketplaces, 37–38, 71

Gravitation, 164

Great Game of Business, The (Stack), 140

Groundhog Day (movie), 79

Groundhog Day effect, 79, 135

Groupthink, 231–32, 237, 246, 266

Growth

    engines of. *See* Engines of growth

    nonlinear, 85–86, 114

    repeatability before, 80–82

    as series of steps, 79–80

Growth rate, 87–89, 101. *See also* 10x strategy

    Facebook case, 92–93

Happiness, 28–29

    Customer Happiness Index, 137–38

    five-step process, 106–10

Happy customer loop, 116–17

Hedlund, Marc, 237

HiPPOs (highest-paid person's opinions), 195, 231

Hockey-stick curve, 22–23, 79–80, 86, 214

"Honeymoon period," 3

Hubbard, Douglas, 197

HubSpot case study, 137–38

Hypotheses

    assumptions turning into falsifiable, 200–201, 206, 213

    learning experiments, 174–75

Identifying constraints, 140, 172–75

    exercise, 158–59

    presprint meetings, 243

IDEO, 231–32

IMVU case study, 155–56

Innovator's bias, 21–22, 258

Innovator's Solution, The (Christensen), 61

Internal constraints, 152–58, 159

    physical, 153–57

    policy, 157–58

Intrapreneurship, 239–40

Inventory, 41–43

Irrationality, 78

Jobs-to-be-done concept, 62

Jones, Daniel T., *Lean Thinking,* 12

Judge, Mike, 212

Kaplan, Saul, The Business Model Innovation Factory, 23

Key performance indicators (KPIs), 8, 9, 238

Kickoff meetings. See Presprint meetings

Knack, The (Brodsky and Burlingham), 53

Lean Canvas, 12, 15–17, 167–68

    curse of specialization, 8

    Mary's business case, 5, 8

    testing/refining business models, 64–68

    traction model versus, 77

    USERcycle case study, 54, 55–56

Lean Canvas case study, 220–27

    activation, 222–23

    analyze, 224, 225–26

    background, 220–21

Scrum/agile methodology, 232–33

S-curve, 86–87

Secondary metrics, 173–74

Sellers, in marketplaces, 37–38, 71

Semiautonomous meetings, 239

Serial split testing, 204

Seven habits counteracting cognitive
        biases, 193–204
    declaring expected outcomes up front, 193
    declaring outcomes as team sport, 194–96
    emphasizing estimation, 196–98
    measuring actions versus words, 198–200
    time-boxing experiments, 202–3
    turning assumptions into falsifiable
        hypotheses, 200–201
    using control groups, 203–4

Sharing economy, 186

Short-list solutions, 235, 246–52

Sierra, Kathy, 28

Singularity moment of product, 95

Skok, David, 89, 118

Skunkworks, 239

Slack (software), 254

Small experiments, testing big strategies
        through, 190–92

Small teams, 237

Smoke tests, 75

Snapchat, 36

Social proof, 131

Socratic method, 259

Software as a service (SaaS), 30, 32, 54, 58,
        62, 65, 90, 180

Solution interviews, 75, 175, 181

Southwest Airlines, 169–70, 172, 176

Specialization, curse of, 8

Split testing, 137, 204, 217, 225, 226

Sprint planning meeting, 229, 246–52
    agenda, 247–52
    attendees, 247
    duration, 247
    purpose, 246

Sprint review meeting, 229, 255–57
    agenda, 255–57
    attendees, 255
    duration, 255
    purpose, 255

Sridhar, K. R., 153

Stack, Jack, *The Great Game of Business,* 140

Staged rollouts, 101
    building out customer factory, 84–85
    Facebook case, 82–84
    repeatability enabling, 77–79

Stand-up meeting, 229, 252–52

Starbucks, 27

Starting constraints, 151, 159

Sticky engine of growth, 119–20

Strategy
    analyze your, 218–19
    definition of, 189–90
    testing through small experiments,
        190–92

Suboptimal experiments, 7, 11–12

"Success theater," 258

Sun Tzu, 189